Welcome

Reflections on a Journey through Cancer
(and a few thoughts on facing your own storm)

Dr. Ted Wueste

Unless otherwise noted, Scripture quotations are from the ESV® Bible (The Holy Bible, English Standard Version®), copyright © 2001 by Crossway, a publishing ministry of Good News Publishers. Used by permission.

Library of Congress Cataloguing-in-Publication Data
Wueste, Ted
Welcome Everything: Reflections on a Journey through Cancer / Ted Wueste
Library of Congress Control Number: 2020919754

ISBN 9780991636860

Printed in the United States of America
First Edition

CONTENTS

You have multiplied, O LORD my God,
your wondrous deeds and your thoughts toward us;
none can compare with you!
I will proclaim and tell of them,
yet they are more than can be told.

Psalm 40:5

"When his longing after a living God is met with the offer of a paltry escape from hell, how is the creature to live? It is God we want, not heaven! God, not an imputed righteousness."

George MacDonald

First Thoughts: Welcome Everything

Welcome everything.

Everything? Well, yes ...

And, to welcome everything, we start with nothing.

In Romans 8, we are told that nothing can separate us from the love of God:

> For I am sure that neither death nor life, nor angels nor rulers, nor
> things present nor things to come, nor powers, nor height nor depth,
> nor anything else in all creation, will be able to separate us from the
> love of God in Christ Jesus our Lord. (vv. 38-39)

Nothing. There is nothing that is able to separate us from God's
love. It is easy for us to slip into a "separational" theology, believing
that God is perhaps more accessible in some situations than others.
We might not verbalize it that way but if we are honest, when going
through difficult circumstances we often say things like "where is
God?" Or, "when is God going to show up?" We generally look at
life through a lens that filters into categories of "good things" and
"bad things." We try to stay away from the bad and multiply the
good.

And, then, we inadvertently put that lens on God as well as our perception of His love and presence in our lives. Romans 8 blows this way of looking at things out of the water. There is nothing that can separate us from God. If we begin to understand God and His love as the "good life," then good circumstances or bad circumstances have no bearing. In that sense, we can "give thanks in all circumstances." (1 Thessalonians 5:19) In all things, in everything.

Everything is a connecting point to His love and experiencing His presence in our loves. Read that again. *Everything*. It might even be said that anything which seems like a separation is actually a place to connect. Simone Weil, the writer and mystic from the early 20th century, wrote:

> *Two prisoners whose cells adjoin communicate with each other by knocking on the wall. The wall is the thing which separates them but is also their means of communication. It is the same with us and God. Every separation is a link.*

There is deep grace in being stripped of associating the "good life" with positive circumstances. When we are feeling empty and perhaps reeling as we walk through a time of suffering, we have the opportunity to embrace that new definition of good. In fact, earlier in Romans 8, we find a verse that says, "And we know that for those who love God all things work together for good, for those who are called according to his purpose." The good? The purpose? Drawing closer to the heart of God.

It is easy to describe but not necessarily so easy to live in this reality. There is often struggle, doubt, and tension along the way. However, we begin with holding that tension and not running away from it.

So, anything we walk through in life is an occasion for drawing near to God, to diving deeper into life with Him. C. S. Lewis talked about the reality that the good life is Trinitarian in nature and it occurs as we draw near to Him that we join in and participate in the life of God:

> It matters more than anything else in the world. The whole dance, or drama, or pattern of this three-Personal life is to be played out in each one of us: or (putting it the other way around) each one of us has got to enter that pattern, take his place in the dance. There is no other way to the happiness for which we are made ... if you want to get warm you must stand near the fire; if you want to get wet you must get into the water. If you want joy, power, peace, eternal life, you must get to, or even into, the thing that has them. They are not a sort of prize which God could, if He chose, just hand out to anyone. They are a great fountain of energy and beauty spurting up at the very center of reality. If you are close to it the spray will wet you: if you are not, you will remain dry. Once a man is united to Christ, how could he not live forever? Once a man is separated from Christ, what can he do but wither and die?" (Mere Christianity)

A friend gave me this reading from Lewis when I was in the hospital being treated for Acute Myeloid Leukemia. I had written in an update that walking through what was one of the most difficult times of my life was stripping me of the life I knew and I could feel God drawing me closer to Him. Rather than seeing this season of suffering as simply a bad thing (even though it was painful and hard), I was beginning to see it as grace. God was leading me through the releasing of my false sense of self, an identity in which my life was built around what I do, what I can accomplish, and what I can produce.

The emptiness I experienced was indeed leading to a place of hunger like I'd never experienced before. Rather than being deflating, it was liberating to think that God was drawing me a place of truly being at rest in Him.

What I began to see was that the emptiness and the seeming meaninglessness was actually leading me to a place of radical acceptance that led to peace in the midst of the storm.

In his classic, *Testament of Devotion,* Thomas Kelley makes the observation that "Nothing matters; everything matters." Only as we are able to say that "nothing really matters" are we able to see that "actually, everything matters." When we are able to see the futility of life, we are then open to experiencing the deeper reality. When we see all the obstacles and the fact that we have been stripped of life as we know it, we are able to rest and walk in peace and joy and power. So many of the promises of Scripture can feel like theory but suffering leads us to a place of knowing them beyond knowledge. (cf. Ephesians 3:19; Philippians 4:7)

For this paradox of nothing and everything, Kelley goes on to share: "It is a key of entrance into suffering. He who knows only one-half of the paradox can never enter that door of mystery and survive."

Suffering is indeed a paradox. It is an experience that we usually seek to push away but the sufferings of life are unavoidable. So, trusting that God is at work in all things, we can embrace our sufferings. And, we can actually welcome them. Richard Rohr, in his classic work, *Everything Belongs*, writes:

> *Everything belongs and everything can be received. We don't have to deny, dismiss, defy, or ignore. What is, is okay. What is, is the great teacher. I have always seen this as the deep significance of Jesus' refusal of the drugged wine on the cross.*

Because *everything can be received*, we can pray a prayer like this which has been attributed to Thomas Keating:

> *Welcome, welcome, welcome. I welcome everything that comes to me today because I know it's for my healing. I welcome all thoughts, feelings, emotions, persons, situations, and conditions. I let go of my desire for power and control. I let go of my desire for affection, esteem, approval and pleasure. I let go of my desire for survival and security. I let go of my desire to change any situation, condition, person or myself. I open to the love and presence of God and God's action within. Amen.*

Notice the pattern: welcome, let go, and open.

In the following pages, I share theological reflections that were shaped during my days of walking through Hodgkin's Lymphoma, a recurrence of Hodgkin's Lymphoma, Acute Myeloid Leukemia, and then a stem cell transplant. I share how God shaped me by offering *current reflections* (set apart by chapter titles) as well as *updates* from a blog that I wrote during these years (these entries have dates setting each section apart). You'll read several entries from my beloved bride, Jenifer, in the second year of these updates.

My prayer as you read is that you would stop and talk to God when you notice the Holy Spirit nudging your spirit in order to meet with God in these pages.

Let's do that right now. Take a few moments and consider where you find yourself right now. Are you in the midst of a storm? Are you facing things are that uncertain? Stop. Be still. Talk to God about it.

No, seriously! If you haven't, be still for at least a few moments and know that He is God. Express your heart and your hopes to God as you begin reading these pages.

Before, moving on, sit with these words from Henri Nouwen:

> *Suffering invites us to place our hurts in larger hands. In Christ we see God suffering, for us. And calling us to share in God's suffering love for a hurting world. The small and even overpowering pains of our lives are intimately connected with the greater pains of Christ. Our daily sorrows are anchored in a greater sorrow and therefore a larger hope.*

1

When the Student is Ready ...

Along with welcoming, let me share one more thing before we start this journey together.

There is an old saying that goes something like this, "When the student is ready, the teacher appears." We can welcome everything because everything can be our teacher. Not teaching us "lessons" as though in need of more information. If that was the case, we could argue for a pain-free, blissful existence with the help of a stack of great books. The teaching that can happen through a time of suffering is learning to love and be loved. You can't learn that in a book.

The reason I bring this up is because you are *ready*. If you find yourself in season of suffering, it most likely does not feel like you are ready to walk through it. It may not feel fair. You are likely experiencing myriad emotions, grappling with the wrongness and unjustness of it all. However, right alongside all these normal responses are realities deeper and truer than our imaginations can hold. If you are in Christ, you have everything you need. And because we have everything we need in Christ, we are ready to learn how to welcome everything that we encounter in life.

We often hear people talk about asking for blessings but we have been "blessed with every spiritual blessing in the heavenly places." (Ephesians 1:6) Or, perhaps there is a feeling that we need more but "His divine power has granted to us all things that pertain to life and godliness, through the knowledge of him who called us to his own glory and excellence, by which he has granted to us his precious and very great promises, so that through them you may become partakers of the divine nature." (2 Peter 1:3-4)

Partakers in the divine nature? Yes. We share or partake in the life of God. God is love (1 John 4:8) and that is lived out in fellowship between Father, Son, and Holy Spirit. We are invited into the circle. Indeed, we are in that circle but it is possible that we haven't fully embraced that reality.

Take a few moments and sit with that. Let the reality, that God not only loves you but He (Father, Son, and Holy Spirit) holds you in His love, settle in your soul. And not only that, Romans 5:5 describes more of this reality: "God's love has been poured into our hearts through the Holy Spirit who has been given to us."

The German mystic, Hildegard of Bingen, wrote: "You understand so little of what is around you because you do not use what is within you."

So, you may feel like you are not ready. You may feel like you don't have what it takes to walk through a time of suffering, a storm. You may feel defeated. You may feel all kinds of things.

And, here is the reality: in Christ, you have the resources to walk through anything. Maybe, just maybe, as you walk this path, your awareness will grow and you'll begin to experience the depths of who you truly are in Christ ... in ways far deeper and more profound than you've ever imagined. The thing that you've thought might destroy you is actually what delivers you into a deeper, more intimate, more life-giving relationship with God.

In Philippians 1:28-29, there is a fascinating encouragement from the Apostle Paul to the follower of Jesus in Philippi. He wrote:

> *and not frightened in anything by your opponents. This is a clear sign to them of their destruction, but of your salvation, and that from God. For it has been granted to you that for the sake of Christ you should not only believe in him but also suffer for his sake.*

First, we see the encouragement to not be frightened in the face of suffering. That sounds nice, but why? Why not be frightened? The text goes on to say, because this is a sign of their destruction. What is "this?" The suffering. And then, it is important to note that the word "their" is not present in the original Greek writing. It could more accurately be translated, "to them, a sign of destruction, but to you a sign of salvation."

When the word "salvation" is used in Scripture, we always have to stop and ask, "salvation from what?" Salvation can refer to being saved from physical harm, saved from the consequences of sin, saved from the presence of sin, or saved from power of sin in our lives. Sin, put simply, is the reality of living independently of God. It can result in "sins" which are the fruit of living in my own power, strength, and wisdom. In this context, the salvation being described is being delivered from an independent way of living. Suffering does that. Suffering, the text goes on to say, has been "granted" (or, graced) to us.

So, here's the point: what looks like destruction to some is, for a follower of Jesus, actually a sign that His grace is at work. The text goes on to say that it has been "granted" (or, graced) that we would not only believe but also suffer for His sake. In our union with Christ, suffering is a grace.

Again, sit with that for a moment: a grace? a gift? Really? Yes, really. God is always in the process of loving us and saving us. He is always in the present and at work in our lives. His heart is that we would grow closer and closer to His heart ... that the weeds in our lives would die away and the roots of our soul would grow deep into Him. Suffering has a unique way of sifting and sorting the weeds from the roots of the life we have in Him.

So, we can say, as we are entering into a storm and as we are in the middle of it, "God is saving me."

An unknown author imagined a conversation that we might have with God:

Me: Hello God.
God: Hello...
Me: I'm falling apart. Can you put me back together?
God: I'd rather not.
Me: Why?

God: *Because you're not a puzzle.*
Me: *What about all the pieces of my life that fall to the ground?*
God: *Leave them there for a while. They fell for a reason. Let them be there for a while and then decide if you need to take any of those pieces back.*
Me: *You don't understand! I'm breaking!*
God: *No, you don't understand. You're becoming. What you feel are growing pains. You're getting rid of the things in your life that are holding you back. The pieces are not falling down. The pieces are being put in place. Relax. Take a deep breath and let those things you no longer need fall down. Stop clinging to pieces that are no longer for you. Let them fall. Let them go.*
Me: *Once I start doing that, what will I have left?*
God: *Me.*
Me: *I'm afraid to change.*
God: *I keep telling you: You're not changing, you're becoming.*
Me: *Becoming who?*
God: *Becoming who I created you to be! A person of light, love, charity, hope, courage, joy, mercy, grace and compassion. I made you for so much more than those shallow pieces you decided to adorn yourself with and that you cling to with so much greed and fear. Let those things fall off you. I love you! Don't change! Become! Don't change! Become! Become who I want you to be, who I created. I'm gonna keep telling you this until you remember.*
Me: *There goes another piece.*
God: *Yes. Let it be like this.*
Me: *So... I'm not broken?*
God: *No, but you're breaking the darkness, like dawn. It's a new day. Become!! Become who you really are!!"*

God never promises to keep us away from suffering but He does promise Himself. The reason that we can gently release our fears and perceptions is because God is with us. He promises to never leave us or forsake us.

The Psalmist repeats a statement several times and the author of Hebrews picks it up as well: *The Lord is my helper; I will not fear. What can man do to me?*

So, as we begin this journey together, remember that "when the student is ready, the teacher will appear." The fact that the teacher (in the form of a season of suffering) has appeared is a reminder that you are ready. And you are ready, not because of you, but because Christ is with you, loving you, walking with you.

I had not been feeling well since Labor Day. What I thought was perhaps a sinus infection lasted for several weeks. My first visit to the doctor was on September 28th. I was diagnosed with bronchitis and sent home with some medications. While I was taking the medications I felt great, but as soon as I stopped taking the medications, my fatigue and difficulty breathing returned. After three more weeks of trying to treat my symptoms with little relief, it became clear to me that something more was going on. I returned to the doctor. He didn't have any answers but after I requested it, he agreed to order a chest x-ray just in case.

A week later, he called and said that the x-ray showed a shadow that needed further exploration with a CT scan. I had the CT Scan on Friday, October 27th. On Monday October 30th, I received a call from my primary care doctor who said I had a 3.5-inch mass in the middle of my chest and that it appeared to be lymphoma. He immediately referred me to an oncologist. After a good cry with Jenifer and some prayer, I made an appointment with the oncologist for Friday, November 3rd.

The oncologist agreed that the probable diagnosis was lymphoma but more tests needed to be done to be sure. I asked her if the 3.5-inch mass was pretty big and she simply answered, "I've seen bigger." It seemed clear that we needed to move quickly into whatever was next. The next step was blood work and a biopsy. The oncologist immediately sent me to a surgeon for an ultrasound to see if they could do a biopsy of a lymph node in my neck or underarm. Unfortunately, that was not possible. So, I was scheduled for a CT-guided needle biopsy of the mass in my chest on Monday, November 6th. My oncologist called me the next day with the results: lymphoma. The needle biopsy was able to confirm the lymphoma diagnosis; however, the sample was not enough to determine the type of lymphoma. This is needed to determine the specific treatment. My oncologist has been great about getting appointments, tests, and results very quickly for me.

Next, I was referred to a thoracic surgeon because I will need a more invasive surgery to get a larger sample of the mass. The surgery will be done under general anesthesia and I will likely have to stay in the hospital overnight for monitoring. I will have the surgery on Monday November 13th.

These are the facts of the circumstances in which I find myself today. *However*, there are deeper, truer realities that are guiding my heart and my mind ... I have a relationship with the God of the Universe who is lovingly, graciously, and sovereignly present with me. I know that my life is not my own and so I trust Him to guide this process with all the love, grace, goodness, and holiness that mark His character. I also know that the deepest need in my life is to receive His love and share it with others, and there is nothing that can separate me from His love (Romans 8). This is a circumstance in which I will experience His love in new ways and I look forward to that. Already, I see beauty all around: a wife who is the most amazing companion I could ever ask for, kids who love me, and a community with whom I get to connect more frequently and journey together in prayer. These are all deep joys in the midst of a hard situation. Thank you for desiring to journey with me in this ...

Sunday, November 12   **Surgical Biopsy**

Hi praying friends ... the surgical biopsy is scheduled for 4:30pm on Monday Nov 13. Pray that the least invasive option produces good material to get a proper diagnosis. We'll let you know how it goes!

Thankful that He holds all of this ...

> *So, we do not lose heart. Though our outer self is wasting away, our inner self is being renewed day by day. For this light momentary affliction is preparing for us an eternal weight of glory beyond all comparison, as we look not to the things that are seen but to the things that are unseen. For the things that are seen are transient, but the things that are unseen are eternal. 2 Corinthians 4:16-18*

Monday, November 13   **Post Surgery**

Quick update ... surgery went well with the least invasive option. Recovering well and looking forward to sleeping well tonight. Thanks for all your prayers!

Tuesday, November 14   **Biopsy Update**

The surgeon said that he was able to get two samples that were both about the size of dice. The pathologist said that the samples were a good size. The only challenge is whether or not they are good samples. The samples could be "necrotic" (dead cells) and the surgeon said that at least parts appeared to be so. If fully necrotic, they'll have to do another surgery. We should know in 3-5 days. If the last biopsy was any indication, our oncologist will be aggressive and we might know sooner.

So, thanks for your prayers and keep praying that the pathologist would have something with which to work!

I'm resting today at home - feeling like I got punched in the throat ... partially from the intubation and partially from the incision just above the sternum. Now, I know why they call it "fighting" cancer ... you can feel like you got in a fight! Well, I'm getting back up in His strength, seeking Him today and desiring to be attentive to His presence and love for me. Thanks for being the hands and feet of Christ in my life. I do not feel alone.

More than anything, pray that I would not attach certain outcomes or expectations to His love for me but rest in the reality that He is a good Father who will never give me a stone when I ask for bread! (cf. Matt 7)

Thursday, November 16   **Biopsy Results and Next Steps**

Thank you again for all your prayers and love. I want you to know that I read each comment, prayer and encouragement that you leave here. I may not respond to your comments but I see them all and they mean a lot.

This morning, the oncologist called with a preliminary report: Hodgkin's Lymphoma. The stage will be determined after a PET Scan tomorrow and looking at some other factors. I presently have several extra risk factors: male, older than 45, and the presentation of some "B" symptoms. Starting treatment quickly will be important. Tomorrow will start 4 days of tests and procedures to get ready for treatment which will include chemotherapy and perhaps radiation. We will be looking at all the options and have a great team in place to determine next steps and best treatments.

Please keep praying and thanking God. Thank Him that I only had to have the least invasive biopsy. Praise Him that the pathology report came quickly. Praise Him that we have an oncologist who is on the ball and very caring. Praise Him that we have the opportunity for and access to great treatments. I got to meet with a great friend who is a nurse navigator for cancer today to walk me though all that is coming my way. Praise Him that we have a great team in place for my care - the first of which is the best wife in the world, truly. Praise Him that He is present and hold all of this in His powerful hands.

Also, I just want you all to know that my hope is not in statistics or risk factors or a favorable prognosis. God is bigger and stronger than all of that and my life belongs to Him so I will seek to "dwell in the house of the Lord" - that is the One thing that I ask (Ps 27). Pray that with me - will you?

And, finally, I want you all to know how thankful I am for you. I feel so supported and held by God in all of this and I know that your prayers are His gracious invitation for you to hold me with Him. So, our prayers are a part of what God is doing in my life. It is a glorious mystery that I don't understand but I am thankful. His goodness is so evident to me in all of this and He is so much better than my mind can comprehend. His peace and love are beyond my comprehension but experienced as deep rest.

I cried for a while this morning as I got the news from the oncologist and I feel emotional even now as I type but right next to the grieving (because life shouldn't be this way) is a deep sense of rest in our good God who is more real to me than ever before and more gracious than I could have imagined. As you can tell, He is doing deep work in me and I am grateful.

This quote has been an encouragement to me in the past and especially now as I walk through a process that will not be quick or easy but will take me deeper with Him.

> "Why am I in such a hurry to arrive? Yet how is it that, I'm grateful for this long and dusty road that is leading me back to loving union with my creator with my beloved. Above all, trust in the slow work of God. We are quite naturally impatient in everything to reach the end without delay. We should like to skip the intermediate stages. We are impatient of being on the way to something unknown, something new. And yet it is the law of all progress that it is made by passing through some stages of instability— and that it may take a very long time."
> Pierre Teilhard de Chardin

2

Hope

Am I going to be okay? What is going to happen to me? Early in a cancer diagnosis, these are some of the questions that pop up. Sometimes with a lot of energy behind them and sometimes it can be more subtle. There are always questions none the less.

When the questions come, they are an attempt to find hope. The questions can even be a form of grasping, trying to find anything to answer the hope question ... trying to find anything to deal with the uncertainty.

Hope.

To live, we need hope. It is air to the lungs of our soul. It is water to a thirsty body. It is a non-negotiable. If we don't have hope, we feel like giving up.

Jesus was asleep in the boat when a huge storm threatened the boat in which He and the disciples were travelling. In Luke 8, we are told waves crashed against the boat, wind swirled about, and water began to fill the boat. Jesus' followers woke Him up and said, "Jesus, we are going to die." He simply replies, "where is your faith?"

Another way that could be phrased is, "in what are you trusting?" Or, "where is your hope?"

As we are confronted with our own storms, it can feel like all the wind has gone out of our sails. We're stuck and our boat might just sink. We might even find ourselves saying some variation of "Jesus, I am going to die," or "I'm not going to make it." As we look at the waves, the wind, and the water, an overwhelming sense of dread can come over us. And, we grasp for something that will tell us everything is going to be okay. In the absence of that, we can spiral.

As we try regain our composure, grasping for false hope is a real temptation. Often, we use statistics or an anecdotal story from a friend of a friend to make ourselves feel better. We google and find out that our form of cancer has a 92% survival rate. Or, a friend tells us that their cousin's best friend took a certain supplement that made his cancer go away without treatment.

We tend to look for hope wherever and however we can find it. The problem with such an approach is that quite often it is just not realistic or consistent with the facts. Desperate people will believe anything if it gives them hope. And, it can provide some comfort to know that only 8% of people with your particular storm die. But, what if you are in that 8%? Ultimately, we can hold on to things like this but they don't end up satisfying. In the depths of our hearts, we all know that at some point we are going to die so pretending otherwise leaves us feeling flat or perhaps even depressed.

Later in my journey through cancer (spoiler alert), when I was dealing with leukemia and right before my stem cell transplant, my wonderful oncologist made a comment that 20% of people don't make it after the transplant. My gut response was verbalized as, "what does that mean?" She gently and graciously said, "It means that 1 in 5 people don't make it past the first year." I think I responded with something like, "Yes, I understand the statistics and percentages but I'm processing what that means." Again, she gently responded with a dose of reality, "If you are in the 20 percent, what this means that we will make you as comfortable as possible and help you with the pain." Ah, reality. There are times when reality smacks us right in the face and false hopes just can't deliver.

The challenge of facing reality also shows up because so many of our friends and family feel uncomfortable when we are going through a storm. They watch, feel helpless, and end up saying things that are not helpful at all. "Everything is going be ok. I just know it." "Just have faith that God will heal you." "Don't worry ..." Next, insert some Bible verse that just sounds like blah, blah, blah as they quote it. This can be discouraging or even deceptive as the discomfort of others lead us into false hope. People generally mean well but guarding our hearts against false hope is so important.

In our soul, we desire real hope ... a real, rooted sense that our lives are not just floating defenseless in the ocean at the whim of the storms that come through.

We want control. We want certainty. We want to know.

Our grasping for these kinds of hope are usually about as successful trying to control a storm. You can't control the weather. You can't control most circumstances at all. So, what hope do we really have? To what can we cling that is true and satisfying? What can anchor us in the midst of the storms?

As we look to God, He doesn't promise we'll never suffer. He doesn't promise that we'll never die. He doesn't promise that everything will turn out okay, at least not in the ways we often define "okay." In the Letter to the Hebrews, the writer uses the visual of an anchor to talk about hope. Hope is described as an anchor for our soul. It is indeed a promise that our soul, our very life, can be secure in the midst of storms. What we desire most is available.

> "We have this as a sure and steadfast anchor of the soul, a hope that enters into the inner place behind the curtain."
> Hebrews 6:19

Often, as people read this verse, the phrase "hope is an anchor" is plucked out and put on a bumper sticker or a plaque. It sounds nice but doesn't tell us the object of that hope. The surprise here is that hope is a person, a relationship. The anchor for our lives is described as entrance into "the inner place behind the curtain." The place behind the curtain is a reference to the curtain which separated the Holy of Holies from the rest of the temple. To be behind the curtain is to be in the direct presence of God. It is an incredibly intimate and personal image that is being painted.

Our anchor, our hope is being with God. It is living with Him as He is with us. Another understanding of this is found in the words of Jesus in John 15 in which He employed the image of the vine and the branches to talk about the abiding life.

He is with us! Augustine made the comment that "He is closer to us than we are to ourselves." There are times when we are intensely aware of this and perhaps more often, there is a need to trust He is present. Especially in a season of suffering, we might not feel it and yet it is gloriously true. It is our hope. Our hope! This anchors us because we are redirected to seeing our lives as rooted in Him, unable to be separated from Him.

This is why Paul writes in Galatians, "Christ in you, the hope of glory." Glory is another one of those words that we think we know what it means but often have a hard time really defining. To make it simple, glory is one's essence. The hope here is that, through the indwelling presence of Christ, we are being shaped into His image or glory. Through our connection with Christ, we are shaped into the image of Christ or the glory of Christ. However, it is not just for the purpose of possessing the character of Christ as an abstract concept. We are being shaped to be like Jesus so we can relate to God the Father like Jesus did. This is a hope that can anchor us.

Jesus trusted in the midst of the storms. He surrendered to God's heart when faced with a brutal death. He looked to the Father because His essence or glory was *connectedness to God*. Our hope is living in this connectedness, trusting that God is at work in us and present with us.

So, as we experience hopelessness, we view as it as invitation to look Godward ... to turn our gaze to Him. It's not about mustering up our own sense of hope or determination. Honestly, in times of suffering, we often have very little strength in ourselves. It begins with remembering that He is our hope. This *remembering* may lead to a *resting* in that reality which may lead to a significant *refocusing* of our perspective.

Often, that process is not so simple but it starts with remembering. And if often continues with remembering again and again. Hope is available and accessible but it usually doesn't come easy or fast in seasons of suffering.

Monday, November 20   **Full Diagnosis and Treatment Plan**

We met with the oncologist around noon today and she shared that I have Classic Hodgkin's Lymphoma and it is Stage 2. Stage 2 means that cancer has been found in more than one spot but all of it is in the upper half of my body. I also had a bone marrow biopsy today and if any cancer is found there, I will be reclassified as Stage 4. The good news is that the doctor believes that it is very, very treatable. We are so grateful.

Tomorrow morning, I go early to the hospital to have a chemo port put into my chest and then I go straight to the clinic to start receiving chemo. The treatment will last around three and a half hours. I will go for treatment every two weeks for 6 months. There will be side effects but the doctors and nurses are optimistic in their ability to mitigate many of the side effects. They encouraged me that continuing to work and do everything I can do is a good thing. Staying active is a part of the healing process.

So, what can I say except that I am grateful for all that God is doing in this ... He is showing me so much of Himself and I am being deeply blessed by you, the body of Christ. Please pray for continued wisdom for the doctors and that I will be a good patient - staying hydrated, taking care of my body, etc.

A song that has been ministering to me deeply these days is "Just Be Held" by Casting Crowns and let me share with you a section of the lyrics:

> *So, when you're on your knees and answers seem so far away*
> *You're not alone, stop holding on and just be held*

Your world's not falling apart, it's falling into place
I'm on the throne, stop holding on and just be held.

I love that idea: my life is not falling apart, it's falling into place!

If I take seriously that God's deepest passion for me is to be more dependent on Him and live in deepening union with Him, then this circumstance will be a way that my life will fall even more into place ... the place of deepening dependence on Him. I'm already enjoying some of the tastes of this and I look forward to more.

3

Identity

When I received the phone call on that Monday morning, it was early ... just a minute past seven o'clock. Jenifer and I were still lying in bed, talking. As the phone rang, I picked it up and didn't recognize the number. "Well, it must be important if they are calling this early." And, then, my doctor said the word "cancer." He shared some other things about meeting with an oncologist that mostly went in one ear and out the other. I was shocked. I was speechless. As I hung up the phone, I looked at Jenifer and we cried together and held each other. *What are we going to do? What does this mean?*

The word "cancer" has almost been elevated to mythical status because of its ability to cast fear, uncertainty, and confusion into even the strongest person. Cancer is no respecter of persons, it hits the wealthy and the poor, men and women, people of all races, and it can be relentless. So, when someone receives a cancer diagnosis, it can be shocking and terrifying and surreal. "Is this really my life?" "Is this really happening to me?"

Here's the thing: we are always telling ourselves a story. We see our lives not as a bullet pointed list of facts but as a story that had a beginning point and is unfolding along the way. We know there will be up and downs but we believe in happy endings. As children, we were read fairy tales and while there is always some sort of conflict, things always end up with the hero winning in the end. For most of us, a chapter called cancer is simply not on the agenda for how our story will be told.

Cancer is just too much.

As we hold the storms of life, how do we make sense of them?

No matter if it is what some might call "treatable" or "the good cancer" (as people insensitively told me about Hodgkin's Lymphoma), cancer is still too much too hold. So, we can feel like what we are experiencing just does not fit in the story. Indeed, we may feel a sense of separation from our own lives, from God. "Is He with me in this?"

We feel alienated from our own story.

In one of his books on contemplation, *Into the Silent Land*, Martin Laird shares an incredibly helpful analogy. He begins with the idea that we often associate our lives with our thoughts, our emotions, our circumstances.

> "The marvelous world of thoughts, sensation, emotions, and inspiration, the spectacular world of creation around us, are all patterns of stunning weather on the holy mountain of God. But we are not the weather. We are the mountain. Weather is happening – delightful sunshine, dull sky, or destructive storm – this is undeniable. But if we think we are the weather happening on

*Mount Zion, then the fundamental truth of our union with God
remains obscured and our sense of painful alienation heightened."*

So, we are *not* the weather. We are the mountain. We are stable and secure in God's love no matter what our thoughts, emotions, and circumstances might be saying to us. "Whoever trusts in the Lord is like Mt. Zion: unshakeable, it stands forever." (Psalm 125:1)

We usually let the circumstances of our lives tell us the story of our lives. Our circumstances become our identity. We say, "I am a teacher." "I am a woman." "I am an athlete." "I am a person who does the right thing." "I am _____."

It's never a good way to live because the reality is none of these things can really tell us who we are. And, when a cancer diagnosis comes our way, it is easy to import that way of determining identity into our journey with cancer. So, we become a cancer patient, or worse, we may think of ourselves as a cancer victim.

For me, I had run over ten marathons since turning 40 and now at the age of 47, I couldn't run. As treatments continued and became more intense, walking down the street for two blocks assisted by my wife was a great accomplishment. Driving to an appointment, I would see someone out for a run and a tinge of jealousy would come over me. It helped that often I just didn't feel like exercising but there was still something in me that identified with being active and able. That was just me, it was my story.

The reality is that it was only a part of my story, really just a detail along the way. Not ultimately important and not the core of who I am. The deeper reality is that I am the mountain. I am beloved by God. I am His beloved. That is the core. That is unshakable. That is something that no circumstance can ever change.

It is important not to deny the reality of the weather. A storm coming may mean I need to seek shelter or close the windows, but the weather can never tell me who I am. So, I can move into a place of saying, "I am the beloved of God who happens to be walking through a cancer journey at this time." Or, "I am the beloved of God and today I happen to not feel well." As we are able to move away from identifying with the weather (the storm), we can identify more deeply with being the mountain.

It is God who is the protagonist in our story. And, it is a good story because we are His beloved. In many ways, we are along for the ride, watching and observing what He will do next. When we are the protagonist in the story, we often get stuck in trying to achieve certain outcomes and we feel the stress of needing things to turn out a certain way. When He is the main character, we can live on that mountain with Him (safe, secure, loved).

The other place where a misunderstanding of identity can show up is with others. People might refer to us as a cancer patient or see us through a certain lens. During treatment, I remember walking into the pharmacy, wearing a mask over my face and I received interesting looks from people (this was pre-COVID 19). Kids usually wear their thoughts on their face and the quizzical looks told me everything, *what's wrong with you?* In those moments, I so wanted to explain things as a way to say, "This is not who I am!"

These struggles with identity are difficult but God uses them to shape us, to lead us into seeing that our lives are more than our circumstances ... our identities are more than what we do, what we have, and what others think of us.

Like a rainstorm that clears the air of pollution and leaves a beautiful clear sky the next day, storms in our lives can clear the pollution from the atmosphere of our lives.

Putting things into context: cancer is not the story. It is a detail in the overall story.

November 22   **Chemotherapy, Part 1 (is in the books)**

One chemo infusion finished! That was my first thought as the nurse pulled the needle from my newly installed port. And now, I don't have to see any doctors, hospitals, clinics, needles, etc. for 16 days!!! It will be a nice break after 15 appointments, procedures, surgeries, tests, and chemo in a span of 17 days.

So, I simply want to give you a short update and again let you know how thankful I am for your prayers and support. I feel it and experience your love. In the midst of "not fun" circumstance, His gifts are shining so brightly and His presence is so rich. And, you are a part of that.

Pray for these coming days. While the first day or two after chemo aren't too bad (just a bit of nausea and some sleeplessness last night), the other days are pretty unpredictable through days 5-6. We'll see what happens. One thing I know is that He is holding me through whatever comes and the darker the night, the brighter His presence will be for me.

One last thought (I can't help sharing all the things that He is bringing to my heart and mind these days) ... the 16th century theologian Ignatius of Loyola wrote this: "We should not prefer health to sickness, riches to poverty, honor to dishonor, a long life to a short life . . . Our one desire and choice should be what is more conducive to the end for which we are created."

Of course, our "created end" is to know Him and dwell with Him no matter the specific circumstance because He is our only true joy. Of course, on a lower level of desire, I prefer health but the lack thereof is making me realize even more that my deeper, truer, more faithful desire is to dwell with Him (Psalm 27).

Love you all - thanks for reading ... I may have fewer updates in the days ahead (I hope so) but I'm thankful to know that I have a community walking with me.

Monday, November 27   **Post Round One of Chemo**
I can't say it enough, thank you. Thanks for your prayers, phone calls, cards, meals, encouragements, etc. I am so graced by a loving community who cares deeply.

So, first - some good news: I received a call today that the bone marrow biopsy was negative. No cancer in the bone marrow! I am so thankful. So, this Hodgkin's Lymphoma is squarely in stage 2.

Next, how have things gone with the effects of chemo? The first few days were ok and then day 5 (last Saturday) was tough. Today (Monday) was not great either. The primary symptoms I'm dealing with are nausea, fatigue, aches, and mouth sores. I'm managing the symptoms as best I can (living with the world's best nurse is grace) but sometimes it can be a little discouraging. Also, I'm not sleeping well. That was to be expected with the steroids in the chemo treatment but the last night or two has been uncomfortable.

In all of this, I'm realizing what a comfort "junkie" I am. Having never dealt with serious illness previously, I find myself identifying with those who suffer physically like never before. There is a gift in that (I trust) even though it might not feel like it in the moment.

All in all, please pray that I take care of myself and rest when I need it. Pray for healing. And, more than that - pray that I abide with Him even when everything in my body is screaming for relief. One of the things that I've experienced in the middle of the night is that the Spirit graciously reminds me who I am and that He is truly all I need. He can meet every need in the midst of the pain or discomfort. My sense of dependence is so heightened right now and while I wish the present circumstances weren't the source of my awareness, it is grace to know and feel and experience my neediness. "Blessed are the poor in spirit." I have found myself challenged so many times in the last week with this realization.

A friend shared this with me last week and it has been a source of meditation over this last week: "Yet hope returns when I remember this one thing: The Lord's unfailing love and mercy still continue, fresh as the morning, as sure as the sunrise. The Lord is all I have, and so in Him I put my hope." (Lamentations 3:21-24 GNT)

Ah, such rich truth ... He is my hope. And His love and presence and grace never stop.

4

"What do you want?"

When many think about the ministry and life of Jesus, one of the prominent elements that comes to mind is His ministry of healing. Jesus healed people with diseases. He healed people who were blind. He healed those who couldn't walk. Two features of His healing ministry are often overlooked.

First, Jesus did not heal every person that came His way. In Mark 1, the text says that He was healing people and the "whole city" came out to see Him. In this situation, Jesus slipped away and went out into the desert. He got away from it all. When His perturbed disciples, who apparently loved all the crowds and healing, found Him, they said, "Everyone is looking for you." Jesus responded, "Let's go somewhere else to preach the gospel, for that is why I came out." Likely, this is a reference to both His ultimate purpose for coming into the world and also why He retreated from the crowds. So, we don't have guarantees that we will be healed when faced with difficult circumstances.

Second, in most situations of healing, Jesus asked a variation of this question, "What do you want?" Clearly, Jesus wasn't asking the question for himself as though He didn't know. In most cases, the need would have been apparent to all: a person couldn't see or someone couldn't walk.

So, why does He ask, "what you do want?" Because Jesus desires to go deeper with us than even the desire to be made well. Consider the words of pastor and author Adele Calhoun as she discusses this:

> "Jesus doesn't grant requests like a genie in a bottle. He works with people, allowing their desires to draw him into the core conversations of life. For Jesus, requests for water, healing, rest, vindication, approval, status and so on all engage soul hungers. Misguided, self-destructive, true or addictive desperations and desires opened doors to relationship."

There is a significant dynamic to notice here. As we draw near to Jesus for healing, He wants to use the opportunity to search our hearts as we answer the question, "what do we want?"

Jesus is capable of healing and He often does so even today. Sometimes, He doesn't. There is deep mystery in trying to understand when, how, and where Jesus heals. Certainly, there are not answers to those questions and most attempts to answer with anything concrete are not consistent with what we know about the nature of God as He has revealed Himself.

The one thing I do know for sure is that Jesus will almost always wait long enough to heal us (if that is indeed His plan) to lead us into a place where we will take a real look at our hearts. He desires that we deeply reflect on the nature of desire.

So, what happens in these moments when we ask that question ("what do I want?") with the Spirit? We begin to notice all the surface desires we have and we become more and more aware that what we desire most is God Himself. Desire for God is what makes us human. In his book *Soul Making*, Alan Jones makes the profound statement that *"A human being is a longing for God."* Not that we *have* a longing but that we *are* a longing. In asking what we desire and long for, Jesus is challenging us to get in touch with the depths of who we truly are and what makes us human.

This simple statement has spoken to me and then sustained me during my years of cancer of treatment. Again and again, I returned to that statement and it has led me to the question: What is it that I truly desire in life? This is now a question I ask myself every day. I ask it in prayer. Beyond good health and a pain free existence, *what I want is God.*

Suffering has a way, as Calhoun suggests, of getting us to look at our hearts and embrace that reality. When we are laid bare with seemingly little worldly hope, the deep gift and grace is to connect with the reality that what we want and who we are, deeper than all else, is God Himself.

And so, that is the beauty of asking, "what do you want?" Desires get sifted and a detachment can occur. Often the word detachment is used in a negative way meaning that we've disconnected from important things. However, in the long history of Christian spirituality, detachment has been used to discuss the idea of disconnecting from things we should disconnect from so that we can attach to things that matter most and are connected to the heart of God. Another way to think about detachment is surrender, we surrender to reality as it is. No longer trying to control or manage or change, what can result is an acceptance (not in a defeatist or "giving up" kind of way, but in a peaceful coexistence). We can coexist with difficult things. They do not have the final say when it comes to who we are, how we view the world, or how we live in the world.

As we release and detach, we move from giving our energy to things outside our control and invest our energy in things that are at the core of reality: God and His heart, His purposes, His goodness. The most significant place where this surfaces in a battle with cancer is in releasing outcomes. It is easy to put all of our focus on the future and what might or might not occur. However, as we are able to release those things, we can stay rooted in the present moment. From the present moment, what can put our focus on what today requires. And, the beautiful irony is that as we embrace the reality that tomorrow is not promised, we are freed to love - to love the person in front of us, to love our family (saying the thing we can no longer wait to say), to love God.

In addition, as we are freed to pay attention to the most real and true desire, we are freed to see what is right in front of us. We see the gifts of the present moment. Even in a hospital room, connected to tubes and lines, we can see the beauty of the nurse who is working so hard to provide for her two teenage kids as a single mom, working the night shift so she can be at home during the day when they get home from school. We can see the beauty of having access to health care when so many don't have that access. We can see the beauty of a God who uses all things to draw us closer to His heart.

In 2 Corinthians 4:16-18, we read:

> we do not lose heart. Though our outer self is wasting away, our inner self is being renewed day by day. For this light momentary affliction is preparing for us an eternal weight of glory beyond all comparison, as we look not to the things that are seen but to the things that are unseen. For the things that are seen are transient, but the things that are unseen are eternal."

We do not lose heart because our hearts are settled into the reality that what we want is Him, and all these afflictions are actually being used by God to root us more firmly and deeply in our life with Him, not just in the future, but right now.

Romans 8 is a chapter of the Bible to sit with and mediate upon during days of suffering. A verse that often gets plucked out from the middle of those words is verse 28. It reminds us that God works all things together for good. Taking that verse without the surrounding context can lead us into a shallow understanding as well as defining good for ourselves. As we discussed before, the "good" is ... being shaped into the image of Christ. Why? So that we are like Him, most significantly like Him in the way He relates to the Father.

To get what we truly want, we have to walk through suffering when it comes our way – staying present to what is. Avoidance and denial move us into fantasy rather than a rooted, real place where we experience God and all His goodness and gifts.

Later in my journey (warning: spoiler alert), as I received the news that the cancer came back, I drove home from an appointment with a surgeon who would be performing another biopsy and I prayed, "Okay Lord, if this is it, if this is just a long good-bye, I accept it. I surrender to your will." And I began to cry, deep sobbing cries. "Lord, it is ok if you take me but I want to live for my wife and kids. My life is yours and I trust you with their story but I don't want this to be their story."

It was actually an incredibly purifying, focusing moment for me. In surrendering, in telling God what I desired, I found a depth in me that don't believe I'd previously experienced.

Years ago, as I met with a spiritual director, we discussed discerning the presence of God, and she said, "His presence in this life is real, and He most often comes dressed as thirst." Many will say the presence of God means the satisfaction of thirst, and in some ways that is true. However, perhaps when we are most alive, desire and thirst is most real to us. The Psalmist declares, "O God, you are my God: earnestly I seek you, my soul thirsts for you." (Psalm 63:1)

Rather than denying desire, cultivate it. Live it.

You see, I want a lot.
Maybe I want it all:

the darkness of each endless fall,
the shimmering light of each ascent.
So many are alive who don't seem to care.
Casual, easy, they move in the world
as though untouched.
But you take pleasure in the faces
of those who know they thirst.
You cherish those who grip you for survival.
You are not dead yet, it's not too late
to open your depths by plunging into them
and drink in the life
that reveals itself quietly there.

Rainer Maria Rilke, *Book of Hours*

Thank you for your prayers and encouragements. The last week, I have felt great. Except for a bout with a fever of 101 on Sunday night, I've felt incredibly normal over the last week. Tomorrow, December 8, I go for chemotherapy round 2. It should start around noon. The chemo session itself isn't stressful but thinking about the days that will follow are bringing me some stress. My life mantra has tended to be "everything is fine" or "everything will work out." One of the things I've been confronted with in these last weeks is that there are times when things aren't fine and things aren't working out (not that there isn't the potential in God's plan for me to have great days ahead!). This is one of those times and it puts stress on my body and spirit. Acknowledging this has not been easy for me as I like to think that stress can't affect me. God has been meeting me in this place of stress and encouraging me to feel what I feel so that I can trust Him with it. There's no room for trust and faith in denial. Once again, He faithfully meets me in places of weakness. I have no doubt that your prayers are being used by our gracious God.

Also, after meeting with my spiritual director this week, I am beginning to embrace that this is a season of limitations and this is not easy for me either. I need to embrace each day - whether a hard day or a good day and simply embrace the gifts that God has for me in that day. Truly, I can't worry about tomorrow because I don't know what it will bring. What a gift to get to live into the words of Jesus in Matthew 6.

So, please pray that I will entrust my stress to our faithful, kind, present God. And, pray that I live into each day, not worrying about whether the next day will be good or bad and not assuming what it will be either.

Sunday, December 17   **Update**

Hi Friends, as always - thank you!! I continue to be supported through your prayers and your reaching out to me with texts, phone calls, emails, cards in the mail, smoke signals, etc. Just wanted to let you know I am grateful.

I also wanted to give you a quick update. The effects of the chemo were definitely more difficult this past week and still lingering a bit. Thankfully, I'll be more prepared next time with some new medications that were prescribed this week. The most difficult thing is that I am tired a lot. If you know me well, you might know that I don't like to sleep - my ideal life would be to sleep 4 hours each night and then have 20 hours each day! So, the Lord is graciously teaching me to release activity (at least as much as I'd like) and accept the limitations that this season is presenting.

As I stop to ponder, I am again reminded of His goodness and faithfulness in the midst of all of this and I want to shout it from the mountaintops ... my life is so full with His grace and glory. It seems that one of the values of suffering is that so much that is inconsequential gets stripped away and seeing substance is so much easier.

Please pray for my next round of chemo which I receive on Friday the 22nd. The toughest days will likely be the 26th and following. I am also starting to lose my hair ... every day a little more comes out. I haven't had to shave my head yet but that might be coming soon! I haven't decided what kind of wig I'll be wearing but I'm leaning toward dreadlocks (that's a joke, maybe).

Finally, I wanted to share about a gift I received this week that means the world to me. First, my friend Tom traveled from Colorado and the spent the day in prayer with me, praying for healing. Second, his wife made a prayer quilt for me that was prayed over by their church. One side is designed to look like a stained-glass window and the other side is a cross. I've now slept under this quilt several times and the symbolism of putting my life, my body under the cross feels so rich to me. Please pray that I continue to remember that I am under the cross.

Grace and love and peace to you all! Merry Christmas and may the riches of His grace flood your heart and mind and body and soul with the peace that passes all understanding.

Friday, January 5   **Update**

Again, I feel like I keep saying this but it is what flows from my heart, thank you - thank you- thank you. Thank you for praying for me and holding me before the gracious God of the Universe! He is so good and faithful to let us be a part of what He is up to - and your prayers are being graciously used by Him.

I am so sorry that it's taken so long for an update. I wanted to update last week but had no energy - I caught some sort of virus that had me down and out over the New Year holiday. Your prayers and antibiotics have me feeling great today. PLEASE pray for Jenifer as she was up all-night last night with vomiting and even passed out. I've got to figure out how to take care of her ... my kids will be a help, for sure.

Good news - the side effects from my Dec 22 chemo were not as bad as the previous treatment. The major issue was blisters on my tongue and soreness in my mouth and a medication helped with that immensely. My next chemo is Monday January 8 and I'll be on a Monday schedule (if all goes to plan) through April 30. Pray that the side effects continue to be helped with the meds I have. So grateful for the people that develop these wonderful, specific drugs that help with chemo!

My hair has continued to thin out and so I have a new haircut. It might not be long until I have the full "bald look." Jenifer says it looks good so that's all I need!

I have to let you know that I am full of so much joy in the midst of this ... some days, the joy feels harder to access but today I am fully experiencing His joy. The main thing I am learning is that vulnerability is a gift. Maybe a better way to say it is that acknowledging my true vulnerability is a gift. When faced with good days, hard days, days when I don't feel like I have anything to offer, I feel the sacredness of being loved by God. To feel that is a gift. To be stripped of my ability to do and achieve is a gift.

I am relishing it even when I feel the tension. Tension is another word for which I am learning to be thankful. The tension between praying "I don't want this illness anymore" and praying "I give You thanks for all things" ... both are true and real (the Psalms model this for us).

So - please pray that I will continue to listen and love well in this present circumstance.

5

Emotions and the Psalms

Uncertainty. Grief. Anxiety. Anger.

In walking through a season of suffering, these words start to scratch the surface of what might be a part of the mix. For some, anxiety becomes a constant companion and for others anger bubbles to the surface over and over again. And then, uncertainty and grief add fuel to the fire. For many of us, these responses are a tag team that won't seem to leave us alone.

Most of us have been taught over the years to get rid of unpleasant emotions. Certainly, many of the emotions that arise in suffering are no fun at all and often feel dark, but is trying to get rid of them the best thing? Based on our upbringing or our temperament, we may have different ways of dealing with what some call negative emotions. However, in the Psalms, we are invited to "feel what we feel."

In fact, we see it modeled over and over again: anxiety, anger, uncertainty, and grief all brought to God in prayer. Emotions are a gift from God. The way we interact with emotions might not be a "gift" but having them is a part of how God designed us. Anger reminds us that all is not right in the world. Anxiety or fear could be a signal that something dangerous is occurring. Uncertainty drives us to look toward what is truly certain and dependable. Grief shows that we value something.

The challenge and the encouragement: bring all of these emotions to God, in prayer. An honest reading of the Psalms, the prayer book of the Scriptures, can be uncomfortable and surprising. For example,

> How long, O Lord? Will you forget me forever? How long will you hide your face from me? (13:1)

> My God, my God, why have you forsaken me? Why are you so far from saving me, from the words of my groaning? (22:1)

> My tears have been my food day and night, while they say to me all the day long, "Where is your God?" (42:3)

> With my voice I cry out to the Lord ... I pour out my complaint before him; I tell my trouble before him. (142:1-2)

So, rather than trying to get rid of unpleasant emotions and responses, the invitation is to bring them to God. The beauty of the Psalms is manifold: the normalization of anxiety and anger, the realization there is a place for uncertainty and grief, and a display of the heart that responds by crying out to God.

Perhaps there is nothing more crucial to deepening our life with God than crying out to Him with all the we are, holding nothing back. We may have been brought up in a tradition that says some things are off limits in our relationship with God, or we may have a temperament that tends toward more calm responses to life. However, the Psalms tells us that everything is fair game in our prayer. Anything is a subject matter for prayer.

If we hold things in or try to "manage" our emotions, we are keeping part of ourselves (and maybe the most significant part of us in the present moment) separate from God. Internalizing or suppressing our "negative" emotions (although I would argue that all emotions are gifts from God) leads to a denial of what is actually our experience. Maintaining this kind of separation keeps us from the one who can truly bring confidence in the midst of anxiety, peace in the midst of anger, trust in the middle of uncertainty, and acceptance as we experience grief.

When we are simply with God, the relational dynamics bring a shift and a transformation. 2 Corinthians 3:18 tells us that we, "beholding the glory of the Lord, are being transformed into the same image from one degree of glory to another." Beholding Him, not trying to hold things together or get into a better emotional state, leads to that shift. As we behold Him with all of who we are and all of what we are experienced, our intimacy deepens.

And, finally, when our journey is public to any degree, it is helpful to know that we may find ourselves in a place of having to respond to the emotions of others. At the time of my initial diagnosis, I was serving as a pastor in a local church and the church walked with me so faithfully and graciously. It was actually quite wonderful. I was working with a pastor who was so incredibly supportive. There are times when he would just come and sit with me in the hospital. Most people were so supportive and encouraging. In fact, one person in our congregation sent me cards and regularly left gifts and notes of encouragement on my doorstep. If it was near Valentine's Day, there might be a gift bag with heart cupcakes, a card with some inspirational thoughts, and a heart decoration to put somewhere in the house. Other holidays would follow suit. To say that I experienced support would be an understatement.

And, there were also a number of people who wanted to give me advice and one person even asked what I had done to get cancer. I had people saying that if I just read a certain book or started using a specific supplement, I could kiss cancer good bye. Another gentleman (I use that word graciously) told me that chemotherapy was of the devil and that I shouldn't give in to the oncologists and big pharma who just wanted to keep people sick so they could make money.

Why is it that people were so ready to give unsolicited advice and why is it that people often assumed that I, as the person with cancer, hadn't done any research or asked any questions?

I believe the answer is fairly simple: it is about fear and control.

People frequently take another person's situation and make it about themselves and their own fear or need to control. Aside from getting cancer because of a lifestyle choice (and that can happen), most of the time there are other factors at work that are beyond our control and usually even beyond our awareness. I was told up front that I didn't do anything to contract Hodgkin's Lymphoma. However, people will believe conspiracy theories and very unsubstantiated medical studies if it gives them a sense of control.

Even more tragic is when a "well meaning" person talks to you about sin and that perhaps sin caused your illness. This is another evidence of a theology of control. It is neither Biblical not logical. Or, another form of trying to get a sense of control can come in the form of statements like: if just pray enough or have enough people praying, then I will achieve some outcome. Prayer is efficacious and I am so grateful for all who prayed for me. However, the effectiveness of prayer is not based on the number of prayers, and the desired outcome is actually to draw near to the heart of God.

Very much in the back of my mind through all of this was my mom who died of cancer when I was thirty-six. She battled so valiantly and tried every kind of therapy and pursued every possible remedy from eating only fresh vegetables to meeting with a faith healer. She was up for anything and sought to trust God step by step. At this point, I am cancer free but I can tell you that it isn't because I have faith or have more faith than others. I don't know of anyone who sought God more fully than my mom and yet she is not here today. The outcomes of current circumstances are in the hands of the Lord. Some experience healing, others don't. However, *all have the opportunity to allow seasons of suffering to draw them deeper in Christ and to mold them further into His image.*

Praying like the Psalmists as we bring it all to Him is part of the mystery of how we participate in what God is doing in our suffering. I don't understand it all but I come, I pray ... and nothing is off limits. This kind of prayer is often gritty and messy.

As a person walking through a journey with cancer, it can be easy to fall prey to conspiracy theories, quick fixes, and cure-alls. The uncertainty of a cancer diagnosis can lead us down the path of grasping for answers. The reality is that we are not in control, the future is uncertain, and we have no guarantees of specific outcomes. We may experience the impulse to try to get rid of uncertainty and the feelings of being out of control, but we have to come to terms with our own mortality and lack of control. The example of the Psalms leads us in that direction.

Monday, January 15   **Finding a Rhythm/PET Scan**

Thank you, thank you, thank you. As I've shared before, I feel surrounded by a cloud of witnesses (you and your prayers) ... and it leads me to "let us run with endurance the race that is set before us, looking to Jesus, the founder and perfecter of our faith, who for the joy that was set before him endured the cross, despising the shame, and is seated at the right hand of the throne of God." (Hebrews 12:1-2)

The other day, I was telling a friend that chemotherapy is a lot like training for a marathon. It is a GRIND. In marathon training, you set out your schedule and you just show up each day for a short run or a longer run of 10 miles, 15 miles or even 20 miles. In terms of schedule, I am now 1/3 of the way through chemo! The finish line is just a few months down the road and I feel like I'm getting my rhythm. When preparing for a long training run, you need to sleep the appropriate amount, eat the right foods (before and during the run), stretch, and then just show up. The run itself can hurt, you might have to walk for part of it, and it might feel discouraging in the midst ... all are a part of the process. In addition, one of the things that I've always loved about running is the long periods of just being with God on one of those long runs. I'm seeking to experience chemo and its side effects in the same way ... opportunities to be with Him, even when I don't feel like it. He is so faithful to be what I need on a given day and to invite me just be what I can. I was supposed to run the Arizona Rock-n-Roll Marathon this past Sunday but had to stop training when I got sick. Hopefully, next year!

This last week of chemo side effects has been the best so far ... still felt like I had the flu for a few of the days but I am finding my rhythm.

This week I have a pulmonary function test and a PET Scan. The pulmonary test is to make sure that the chemo isn't damaging my lung function (it is a possible side effect). The PET Scan will look at the lymphoma and determine if any progress has been made. My oncologist hopes to see a 50% reduction in the tumor as well as the spots in other lymph nodes where cancer was present previously. I hope and pray to be an overachiever! :)
We'll learn the results on Friday.

Friday, January 19   **Good News**
Well, we met with the oncologist this morning and the results of the PET Scan were amazing. The tumor shrunk from 10cm to 4.9cm!! The rest of the cancer in various lymph nodes throughout my body ... gone!!! So, my body is responding to the treatment and we'll continue through the rest of the treatments. God is good and gracious and kind no matter what. If I didn't have good news today, I would still sing His praises for loving me and being with me and maturing my soul so graciously in Him. This is a part of His plan for me right now and I praise Him because He has a plan for my life - not because of good news. Although I must say that I am overjoyed (tears of joy - yes!!!) and I am praising Him and thanking Him. He can heal me in any manner He chooses and it seems that chemotherapy is His preferred method at this point. So, thank You Lord for

modern medicine that You provide because You created people with brains big enough to conceive and develop, etc.

So, please praise God along with me and continue to pray for full healing. Please pray as I have round #5 of chemo on Monday. I start teaching two classes at Phoenix Seminary on Tuesday night and I'm praying for strength and perseverance to teach well.

I continue to lose my hair - a small price to pay ... I've now lost my beard and hair continues to thin!! Love to you all.

Wednesday, February 7   **Day by Day**
It has been several weeks since I've updated and wanted to take a few minutes to share a few things. Again, thank you for prayers. I can feel the support.

In some ways, there is nothing new ... still feeling deep gratefulness for a good PET Scan (thankful that, by God's grace), my body is responding to the treatments. And so, we keep grinding away with the treatments. I still am feeling side effects that week of treatment but last time was the easiest and this week, so far so good. I'm learning that rest is huge and I'm learning to listen to my body!

In other ways, I feel like I am being renewing day by day ... a Scripture that has meant so much to me over the year has taken on new meaning during these days: "So we do not lose heart.

Though our outer self is wasting away, our inner self is being renewed day by day. For this light momentary affliction is preparing for us an eternal weight of glory beyond all comparison." (2 Corinthians 4:16-17)

In the midst of affliction, He is renewing me and changing me. Truly a gift that is weightier than anything. Often, we think of "eternal life" as something that comes after we die but Jesus makes it clear that we experience eternal now. Affliction and suffering are often what brings it out ... if we let it. We can fight difficult circumstances and wait for them to pass or we can entrust ourselves to Him for that renewal that comes day by day.

I've been reading a book called "The Passion and the Cross" and it beautifully illustrates what I've been learning about vulnerability in this season ... here is a sample: "The cross of Jesus doesn't just reveal God as unconditional love; it also reveals how vulnerability is the path to intimacy ... the cross of Christ reveals the God works far differently than do our movies and our imaginations. God never overpowers anyone. Radically, of course, God could. God has all the power. However, God's power to create love and community, paradoxically, works precisely by refusing to ever overpower. It works instead through vulnerability, through something the Gospels call exousia ... the Gospels tell us that when people witnessed Jesus' life and ministry they saw something that sharply differentiated him from others. He spoke with great power, unlike the Scribes and Pharisees. However, they use a curious word to name that power. They never say that Jesus spoke with great dynamism or energy. Instead they use the Greek word, exousia, a word with no English equivalent, but whose meaning can be conveyed in an image: If you would put the strongest man in the world into a room with a newborn baby, which of these two would be more powerful? Obviously, at one level, the man is more powerful - he could kill the baby if he wanted. But the baby possesses a different kind of power, a far deeper one, one that moves things muscles can't move. A baby has exousia, its vulnerability is its greatest power. It doesn't need to out-muscle anyone. A baby invites and beckons and all that's moral and deep in our conscience simple cannot walk away. It's no accident that God chose to be incarnated into this world as a baby." The author goes on to write: "The cross of Christ tells us that at those moments of painful helplessness when we can't impress or overpower anyone, we are acting in a divine way, nonviolently, and in that vulnerability lies the secret to our coming to love and community."

I'm thankful to be pressed in a vulnerable place ... it is teaching me so much about the true nature of God and His goodness. Trey asked if he could sit with me during one of my treatments. What a gift! So thankful for his love and compassion. Every day he asks me how I'm feeling. And again, thanks to all of you for your love and compassion. Your prayers are bearing fruit in my body but even more so in my soul.

6

Vulnerability and Strength

In 2 Corinthians 12, we find what seems like an incredibly paradoxical statement: "When I am weak, then I am strong." We might wrestle with that a bit and then acquiesce to believing that it is true. However, in many ways, it is often left at the level of theory. Going through a time of suffering leaves us weak and vulnerable, and we are challenged to move past theory.

Physical strength often is the first to go. After walking through over two years of back-to-back-to-back cancer therapies and surgeries, I am still trying to regain the physical strength I once had. But even more significant than physical strength is the emotional and spiritual strength that is zapped. Generally, when one area is taxed, the others suffer as well because we are wholistic beings. We have a body, a mind, emotions, and a heart, and together they make up our soul. A final, often ignored, component to our souls is relationships. (see Dallas Willard's writing for more on this)

Taken all together and in context, our souls can indeed become weary, weak, vulnerable. We spend most of our lives living with some sense of strength and invulnerability. When it seems to fade, the disorientation can be fearful and painful.

Yet, the text of 2 Corinthians 12 tells us that when we are weak, we are strong. Understood in context, then, we might actually suggest the converse is true as well: "when we are strong, we are weak." In what sense might that be true? Consider this: when we identify with our strength, we are tempted to live out of that strength and stay in a relational place of independence. This process is so *natural* that we are often unaware. So, when we are weak, that temptation is not present and we are much more disposed to depending on God for strength, wisdom, provision. Perhaps this is exactly why Jesus could say, "Blessed are the poor in spirit" (Matthew 5:3) and "Blessed are the poor." (Luke 6:20)

It is contrary to our natural mindset to think that poverty or weakness in any shape or form would be desired. And, yet, our spirit, renewed in the image of Christ, longs to live out of dependence on Christ. Often, that seems illusive but in a season of suffering, the opportunity for dependence is presented over and over again.

The first impulse with suffering and pain and weakness is usually resistance but what happens when we shift into a place of welcome? Rather than pushing weakness away, what if we embrace it? As we embrace and identify with our weakness and vulnerability, the table is set to enjoy a feast of deepening intimacy with God.

In this way, we can look at what many would view as the worst of times as deep gift and grace. Indeed, 2 Cor 12:9 tells us Paul heard God say to him as he asked for his suffering (thorn) to be removed, "My grace is sufficient."

His grace is sufficient. His love, His presence, a relationship with Him is what we need. This is always true but a season of suffering offers us the gift of living into this reality.

As we become more fully present to this reality of vulnerability and weakness, we start to perceive that strength and safety has always been an illusion anyway. We often carry around a sense of invulnerability until it is taken away from us. To have that veil removed is a deep gift. And then, rather than resisting seasons of suffering, we are able to receive them and walk through them with acceptance and trust and even a sense of joy. Joy ... because we know what happens when we are weak: we experience a true sense of strength in Christ.

At one point during a hospitalization, I was so weak that I could barely get out of bed, I wore diapers, and I couldn't even bathe myself. In those days, Jenifer helped me walk to the shower and cleaned my body as I used what little energy I had to simply hold on to a metal rail on the wall. In our 27 years of marriage, I had never felt closer to her. The depth of intimacy in those moments were beyond my imagination and a deep gift. Meeting one another in vulnerability and weakness deepened our love in ways that years of relating to one another in strength never had.

Perhaps, in a counter-intuitive way, it is weakness that strengthens the bonds of relationship. It is vulnerability that deepens the experience of our union with Christ. Julian of Norwich, the beloved mystic of the Middle Ages, prayed and asked God to give her an illness.

What?

Asking God to give us an illness may seem unhealthy or delusional. What kind of person would do that? Apparently, someone who understood something about her soul and the gift of experiencing God's grace. In Philippians 3, the Apostle Paul asks that he might "share his sufferings, becoming like him in his death." Clearly, there was an understanding in Paul and also in Julian that suffering and vulnerability produced something immensely desirable.

While I don't know that I would ever counsel someone to ask for illness, the idea that someone so desires closeness to God that they would ask for illness speaks volumes and gives us a grid for thinking about our own suffering. One of the realities that I know to be true is that if you haven't experienced suffering, just wait ... you will.

So, what do Julian and Paul have to teach us? Quite simply, that we can hold our suffering without fear and, actually, with deep sense of joy. This might seem incredibly intense and indeed counter-intuitive, and it is both of those things. The struggle to welcome with joy takes us back to the issue of desire. We desire safety and security and strength. Rightfully so. However, rather than seeking those things in and of themselves, the invitation here is find them in God alone. As we release those desires, we are freed to desire God alone and we find a safety, security, and strength provided by God rather than the shifting sand of circumstances. The stance that we take is looking at our suffering and wondering: *God, what are you up to in this? How are you drawing me to a deeper place of dependence?*

As we are able to engage God in this way, we are opened up to wonder and awe. As I walked through treatments, one of the things that I noticed over and over again was that God always seemed to have some surprise, something that I wouldn't have expected. I remember one day receiving an anonymous financial gift, just when we were feeling tight from the constant drain of medical expenses. Or, an old friend from twenty years ago would call just when I needed it.

When we are strong and in charge, we usually miss all these little noticings of God's presence and love. And, when we embrace vulnerability and weakness, we clearly see God's grace. It is always there but when we stop trying to fight for control and strength, our eyes open. And then, our hearts open if we are willing ... if we welcome the suffering and "despise the shame." (Hebrews 12:2)

Monday, February 19   **Please Pray**

Well, friends - I was supposed to be having my 7th chemo treatment this afternoon but instead I'm in the hospital. I had a fever last night that was dangerously high and with low, low white blood cells, I have no ability to fight infection. An ER visit turned into being admitted to the hospital where I will be at least through today.

I know He is in this and I trust, with tears in my eyes, that He is good. This is the week our annual conference with the Spiritual Formation Society and I have been planning my days and trying to be careful so that I would be ready.

Well, I don't know what the week will hold which is ok - it's more than ok because my life and how I serve Him is His business.

Pray for healing and pray for my heart - to welcome what each day will bring as a gift from Him - even when I'd rather have a different gift.

Monday, February 26   **Chemo Day #7**

Well, it has been quite a week. I was supposed to have chemo last Monday but was delayed with a hospitalization from Sunday through Wednesday. Thanks for all your prayers. I was able to get out of the hospital and participate in the Spiritual Formation Society's Annual Conference. It was something that I had been planning for almost two years. What a gift! While still quite weak (walking up a flight of stairs felt like running a marathon) - God gave me the strength to do what was before me. It ended up being a great three days.

I was hospitalized because of a high fever. I know that some have been worried that I caught an infection from someone. Tests revealed that, most likely, I was experiencing high fevers because of my immune system/blood counts being so low. I am still being diligent about not shaking hands and giving hugs but sometimes the body can only take so much. My oncologist commented that I probably just needed the week off from chemo.

So - I go in this afternoon for treatment 7 of 12. I am still finding myself in a thankful place - grateful for the gift of treatments and incredible medical care. In addition, I am finding myself in awe of His love and goodness toward me. In the hospital last week, His love and provision (even when I thought I was going to have to miss the conference) was so thick to me. Thick, like a blanket surrounding me and keeping me warm. Thick, like an inescapable fog that keeps me taking one step at time.

Thanks for walking with me one step at a time ... one day at time --- "why do you worry about tomorrow when today is enough?" Indeed, His presence in my life today is enough.

7

Enough

We are constantly bombarded with messages that tell us that we do not have enough, that we need more. The Gospel tells us a different story. It uses words like enough, sufficient, every blessing, and abundance.

We might be tempted to use those words and apply them to lesser things like circumstances or finances but at the heart of them is truth that He is enough. He alone is enough.

I had the opportunity at the conference I referenced in the last post to teach a few sessions. In one of the plenary sessions, I shared some thoughts on "The Leader's Call." I talked about weakness and vulnerability and said, "my experience of vulnerability was thrust upon me but it is not something that I want to lose. I shared this with my spiritual director last week, and it became very apparent to me that *my greatest fear is that my treatments will be successful and I'll lose this sense of utter dependence. I don't want to go back.*"

Why?

Because I was learning that He was enough. I don't need good health or a full bank account or meaningful work. Those are all nice but I don't need them. To go further, my perception was that if losing this sense of dependence and joy would be the result of getting better, I didn't want to get better. Most of the time, I actually meant this!

I had begun to truly experience that His presence and His love are enough. In the days before that conference (which I was leading as well as serving as one of the plenary speakers), I struggled with being in the hospital and thinking that I might not get out in order to participate. I struggled and then as I took in the reality of the situation, I took a couple of deep breaths and surrendered. I came to the place of genuinely saying: *it's okay. I don't have to be a part of it. Others can take on my responsibilities and make it happen. I am available to God and He is my treasure.*

I was being confronted with the "enoughness" of God in ways I'd never experienced before and the truth was that I found Him to actually be enough for me. I had believed that in theory but now it was real – an experienced reality. And, I didn't want to go back.

Julian of Norwich wrote this prayer: "God, of your goodness, give me yourself; you are enough for me, and anything less that I could ask for would not do you full honor. And if I ask anything that is less, I shall always lack something, but in you alone I have everything." (*Revelations of Divine Love*)

There are moments when we are confronted with or surprised by the enoughness of God. And those moments are grace. They are a gift. We can't produce them. We can only be aware and responsive.

More often than not, we are brought into this awareness when all has been stripped away. When we feel like we have nothing is when we ask, *what is left?* And, the joyous surprise is that we are left with God. His presence. And part of the beauty of those moments is that we see His presence as enough.

Early in my journey, after diagnosis and before treatments began, Jenifer and I were walking through an open-air mall in the evening. We simply wanted to get out of the house and walk, peeking in a few stores here and there. As I walked amidst a crowd of people, all rushing along to buy something or eat something or meet someone, I experienced what felt profound even in the moment. I was intensely aware that I had a baseball sized mass in my chest that, if left untreated, would mean death for me. My mortality and the shortness of life was on full display in my spirit. In that moment, I felt a sense of enoughness: *I've lived a good life. If this is it, it's okay. God is enough for me.*

The juxtaposition of being in a space that was a monument to never having enough was so stark in contrast. God was giving me something that was pure grace: an awareness of enoughness. This would continue to shape and form my spirit in the coming months and years.

In reflection now, I am even more aware that we can't produce those moments, we can simply be open and not fight them as we allow them to drip down into the depths of our souls. Also, as we become aware that our souls are being invaded by thoughts that we don't have enough or that we are not enough, we can recall the truth of our *enoughness* and rest there.

Thursday, March 15 **My New Haircut**

Well - the day finally arrived ... my hair is completely gone! There were a few stragglers but I finally had to clean things up. I laugh and smile when I look in the mirror as I think about how many crazy things I've experienced in these last months. And beneath it all, I continue to experience His goodness and joy. I am still not a fan of chemotherapy or the fact that I don't even have to write my name on the sign in sheet at the oncologist's office (they know me far too well!) but I am deeply grateful that there is truly nothing that can separate me from His love. In fact, being confronted with life not being as it should ends up being a rich invitation to rest more deeply in Him. He is my joy and center, and He is life ... not these circumstances.

And here are a few updates:

1. I finished chemo treatment 8 of 12 last Monday. May 7th will be my last treatment if things continue to go on schedule.

2. I will have a PET Scan next Monday to see how things are continuing to progress. Usually, they don't do another PET Scan until the end of treatment but I asked to do one now. Insurance is paying for it so we're doing it. I'm not worried (truly) one way or other but I started to realize that I'd been planning to be done with all of this in May. So, if things are not progressing - I'd rather know now so I can plan for a different summer. My journey and my life belong to Him and I gladly live in the surrender of that reality, and the love and care of knowing that He cares for me and my life far more than I can imagine.

3. I am continuing to feel pretty great in the midst of all of this ... I definitely have some days that are harder than others and today is a high fatigue day but the side effects have actually lessened through better management of medications and certainly all of your prayers! I am finding myself mentally and emotionally drained as the grind of treatment continues but those are invitations to rest and trust.

So, thanks for all of your love and care and prayers ... I feel and experience those prayers daily.

Saturday, March 24   **Latest PET Scan Results and more**
As always, thank you for your prayers and encouragement. I experience and am rooted in His presence by His grace and through your prayers.

I had a PET Scan on Monday and learned today that there is no cancer anywhere else in my body except the tumor site (which continues to be an encouragement). And the tumor has reduced to 2.9cm. Originally, it was 10cm and after 4 treatments it was 4.9cm. This latest scan was after 8 treatments. Additionally, the metabolic rate (which shows cancerous activity) at the tumor is down to 2.4 and 1.9 is normal. All positive trends.

I am encouraged and thankful. And, I'm putting my hand in His --- trusting that He is walking me forward through the fog. I had a friend ask me yesterday what I am learning through all of this and it feels like I could write a book. At the heart of it, it continues to be grace ... that His gracious gifts just keep coming and an illness or other suffering opens our eyes if we let it. Certainly, we can close our eyes and demand release from the pain, but we can also open our eyes and receive gift after gift. I am choosing (and your prayers help) to keep my eyes open!

Monday, April 23   **Update**

Hi Friends, wow! It has been a month since I posted anything. This is a result of a full last month and feeling great. I am amazed at how our Father keeps telling me ... "I'll provide what you need to serve me." For an achiever type, I often feel like I have to come with my strengths and gifts, and in this season - those feel so lacking and I keep getting "graced" by His presence and provision in my life.

And so, I have found myself helping to lead a 5-day retreat in early April and then speaking at a leadership conference all day last Friday. I continue to teach on Tuesday nights for four hours at Phoenix Seminary. This next Sunday, I have the privilege of preaching at Bethany Bible Church. All are gifts of getting to participate with God in what He is doing in people's lives.

So - thank you for your prayers. I have never in my life experienced the love and care of community as in this season. Thank you! Thank Him for the thickness of His presence in my life and for actually feeling pretty great while I continue to receive chemo. Thank Him that my chemo treatments are nearing the end. Today was the next to last. My final treatment is May 7, and my oncologist won't see me again until the end of June. She is very confident. Thank Him for His goodness and grace in what appears to be my continued healing.

In these days - a few verses from the Message version of Romans 5 have spoken deeply to me:

*"By entering through faith into what God has always wanted to do for us—set us right with him, make us fit for him—we have it all together with God because of our Master Jesus. And that's not all: We throw open our doors to God and discover at the same moment that **he has already thrown open his door to us**. We find ourselves standing where we always hoped we might stand — out in the wide-open spaces of God's grace and glory, standing tall and shouting our praise. There's more to come: We continue to shout our praise even when we're hemmed in with troubles, because we know how troubles can develop passionate patience in us, and how that patience in turn forges the tempered steel of virtue, keeping us alert for whatever God will do next. In alert expectancy such as this, we're never left feeling shortchanged. Quite the contrary — we can't round up enough containers to hold everything God generously pours into our lives through the Holy Spirit!"*

He is meeting me every step with His presence and there aren't enough containers to hold all that He is doing in me. I love these words and they has been my experience - by His grace. I have no guarantees as I move forward except for one thing ... His good presence in my life which becomes richer and more tangible in suffering. It doesn't mean that the suffering is ok or fun or not a big deal but I've found Him to be bigger in the lowest points and I've found Him pursuing my heart when I have a difficult time showing up. Sorry to go on and on but it's difficult when the containers are spilling over.

Finally, and this is something very close to my heart, a dear friend (with whom I get the privilege of training spiritual directors) was in a major car accident the day after our retreat at the first of April. Her name is Christine, she lives in Austin, Texas and is recovering day by day. She has a significant head injury, facial fractures, broken bones, carotid artery damage ... please pray for her. She is so brave and walking with Jesus through this and to have a few more people praying would be a gift to my heart.

Sunday, May 6   **Quick Update**

Tomorrow I head into my last chemotherapy session! I could not be more excited. What a journey this has been over the last six months and you've been a huge part of it. Thanks for your prayers and your love.

After tomorrow, I'll have a PET Scan in the middle of June and we'll see where things are at that point. Things are looking positive but there are never guarantees. So, I am holding it all loosely - knowing that it is in the Lord's gracious, kind hands. I am thankful that I won't have any doctor's appointments for 5 weeks and look forward to that.

So - please continue to pray for healing and that this final round of chemo would melt all the cancer away once and for all. At the same time, please pray that I would draw closer to Him each day because that's what I desire most - more than "sickness or health, poverty or riches, long or short life" (St. Ignatius of Loyola), I desire that I would know Him more fully because "in His presence is fullness of joy." (Psalm 16)

Monday, May 7   **Finished Chemo today**

So - here we go! Thank you for praying with me during these months of chemo. You have been a part of what God is doing, and please continue to pray for healing going forward. Entrusting it all to him ... we'll know more June 15 after a PET Scan.

Tuesday, May 29   **Update**

It has been a quite a month with lots of transitions. I wrapped up my role of Executive Pastor of Spiritual Formation at Bethany Bible Church on April 29. It was a wonderful day in which I got to preach and share my heart one last time. The people of Bethany were incredible gracious to me and it was so much fun to talk for hours at a reception after the second worship service. Thank you, BBC, for the privilege of serving over these last six years. This also marked the beginning of my full-time ministry with the Spiritual Formation Society of Arizona (sfsaz.org). SFSAZ is a ministry that we started 5 years ago and has grown to the point where I needed to invest fully in serving leaders and learners. You can pray as I continue to raise support to do this ministry full time.

Then, on May 7 was my last chemo treatment and now (3 weeks later) I am feeling pretty normal. The side effects are no longer and I am not taking the 10 daily medications to manage everything. I still have a way to go in order to get back my strength and stamina but I am walking every day and trying to get back to where I was a year ago.

Last week, our oldest graduated high school and moved out yesterday. This is a time of joy but also bittersweet because our family is not the same day to day. He will be attending Grand Canyon University and moved in with a group of friends who are all a year ahead in school.

My next PET Scan is June 7 and then I meet with my oncologist on the 15th. I am holding it all loosely, entrusting the results to God's care and the story that He has for me. My prayer is that the cancer will be gone and yet my hope is in His goodness and grace no matter the outcome. I don't share that as a way to "hedge my bets" or prepare for not being let down but my heart is that I am truly entrusting it all to Him. Believe me, I am ready to be done with all the treatments but I want to know Him more than all else so I keep my hope and focus there.

Thanks for praying for me and I pray that I am able to share the news that I am in remission soon.

Friday, June 8 **PET Scan Results**
Yesterday, I had a PET Scan (the first one after finishing chemo). Three hours later, my oncologist called. She said that

something showed up which caused concern and she suggested that I try to get a second opinion with the Mayo Clinic oncologist with whom we met in January.

After further conversations today, what was found is a spot on the mass in my chest. The mass was originally 10cm and it is now down to 2.9cm. There is only cancerous activity showing up in this one spot on the mass. The concern is that the "cancer index" on that spot is higher than the last two scans have shown (3.9 vs 2.4). The expectation is that those numbers would go down, not up. Also, there is uncertainty as to whether or not it is new growth as opposed to the continuation of what was there before.

So, we'll get the consult from Mayo and our oncologist will also consult others. The potential responses are:

- "wait and see if it resolves on its own" because the chemo can continue to work things out
- do a biopsy to confirm what the spot is and go from there/perhaps more chemo or even radiation

I am doing well. When I got the initial call yesterday, I was confused and frustrated. Now, after some time in prayer, I am deeply confident in Him and His provision. I've been praying all along that I want to grow deeper with Him and if this is a part of that, I will approach it with joy and confidence -- knowing that these trials are for His glory in me which is my deepest joy. Please pray for wisdom for the doctors. Pray for healing - I'd love that. But more than anything, pray that I would let Him love me step by step and be my strength.

Right now - my mind is clear (as opposed to the chemo months) and my body feels pretty great (didn't have to take a nap today) and my spirit is at peace.

P.S., I sent this in a text to a friend yesterday and she suggested that I share it: *Right now - there is a lot I don't know so I will focus on what I do know and on the present moment. In this moment, I feel good and I will enjoy that for as long as I have it. I will embrace the vulnerability of the moment because it pushes me to Him and that's a good thing. He is in control and this is His story ... and more than His sovereignty, I rest in the reality that He is so good. There might be tears but I know He is good and if being free of cancer today is not the best way for His goodness to be revealed in me, I can live with that and praise Him with all that I am.*

Thursday, June 28   **Not Great News**

Just when I am getting some hair growing back, I might have to lose my hair all over again.

I have some tough news to share. I talked to the oncologist from Mayo today and after looking at my scans and asking the radiology department at Mayo, he believes that I have a recurrence of the Hodgkin's Lymphoma. He said the scan I had at the end of March seemed to show I was in remission but now it appears the cancer is back! I asked him if this was something he'd seen before and he said that it was not very common but it does happen. So, they will try to do a surgical biopsy (which means going under general anesthesia) if they can, to confirm that it is indeed a recurrence. If not, they'll do another PET Scan in 2-3 weeks. Then, the treatment is 2-3 rounds of chemo (a different regimen than before) and a stem cell transplant/heavy dose of chemo. This does not sound like fun to me!

Thanks for your prayers. I don't know what to ask for, in terms of prayer, but I would love for you to pray ... pray as the Spirit leads. I do know that I want to walk with Him deeply and I want to be formed more into the image of Christ ... other than that, I can't understand what to pray for.

At the prayer garden near my house, there is a quote on one of the stations of the cross that says, "Father, I don't understand you, but I trust you." That's where I am ... I don't understand. It's not an angry or confused "I don't understand" but more of a "this is too much for me to comprehend" kind of thing. So, I am seeking to trust Him. Please join me in that prayer ... that I would live with trust and surrender.

Much love to you all! Thanks for being a part of my team of prayer people. Please share this prayer request with anyone who would desire to pray.

I feel joy and peace and love from the Father in all of this. I also feel sadness and frustration and grief. It is all real and I am seeking to meet Him in each place.

8

Disappointment

I expected after a year of cancer treatment and being given and "all clear" I would be able to get settled back into normal life. And then, only a few weeks later, I received that phone call and heard the news that it looked like my cancer was back. Ah, the deflation I felt was significant. And then, I began to pray, "God, is there more you have for me in this season? Is there more work you want to do in me?" Honestly, I was profoundly grateful for all the ways God had drawn me closer to His heart in the previous year but I was ready to move on. I prayed those questions at first with a bit of sarcasm, but I stuck with those prayers and they moved my heart into a place of trusting that God would use this as He did in the previous year.

Using the word disappointment is perhaps the most descriptive word for what I was experiencing. In many ways, I'd been through enough grief and sadness that anger was not the primary emotion but I had developed a sense of expectation. I expected that things would be different. The doctors had suggested that all was looking good and I'd had several "clear" scans before this most recent one. In a few short weeks, members of our extended family would gather in Hawaii for a bit of a celebration. My hair had started coming back and now this?

In the next year, I would spend over three months in the hospital. In the first six months of that year, I was in a hospital bed more than my own bed. I grew quite close to nurses, doctors, and the amazing housekeeper, Nora, who cleaned my room every day. Nora and I talked about our kids and where to get the best Mexican food as well as her faith. I had deep conversations with nurses in the middle of the night about teenage children who were struggling or marriages that were having a tough time getting off the ground. There were so many beautiful moments of connection.

And, at the same time, I was always ready to get home well before I was released each of the four times I was hospitalized during those months. During the last hospital stay, I found myself getting angry and even a bit depressed. I found myself getting frustrated that I was frustrated.

When my blood counts were in a good place, one of my favorite things to do was to leave the unit I was on and go outside and walk through the cactus garden. The hospital called this "patio privileges" and every day I would ask if today was the day I got patio privileges. One afternoon, I walked outside with my IV pole to the garden and began to cry out to God, "Lord, what is going on with me? Why am I so angry?" It didn't take long for me to sense from the Lord that it was my expectations. I wasn't expecting to have to be hospitalized four times in the first six months of the year. It was not part of the plan! I didn't remember reading that in the brochure.

Expectations.

Gerald May writes: "Expectations are premeditated resentments." I'd wrestled with that statement for years and it came flooding back to me once again. Of course, I was experiencing a bit of resentment and then anger over having to be in the hospital, again. May's statement is a great reminder that we set ourselves up for resentment when we expect things to turn out a certain way.

And that resentment can even escalate to the level of demanding that things happen in a certain way. When it moves to the place of demanding, the anxiety, stress, and anger can shift to palpable levels. The effect on the body as well as the spirit can be significant.

Because we can tend to be outcome oriented rather than process oriented, those demands can shift us away from being present to our body and our spirit. Not attending to our lives, as they are, can move us away from being present to God. Because God is right here with us in the present moment, what is happening here and now is vital. As people of faith, we might be tempted put all of our focus on the future (i.e., heaven) but Jesus didn't speak a lot about heaven at all. He spoke and taught much more about present realities in terms of trust and peace.

One of the beautiful things about the Scriptures is that God gives us pictures of lives where things did not go according to plan. The

Apostle Paul spent so much of his ministry imprisoned or under house arrest. It could have been so easy to wallow in disappointment or even resentment at being put in jail but Paul and other writers of Scripture almost seem to anticipate and expect difficult things. More than that, the deepest value in life is knowing Christ and this speaks of an experiential, "in the course of life," kind of knowing.

> I count everything as loss because of the surpassing worth of knowing Christ Jesus my Lord. For his sake I have suffered the loss of all things and count them as rubbish, in order that I may gain Christ. (Philippians 3:8)

C. S. Lewis speaks of the severe mercy of having expectations and preconceived ideas dashed, and it happens for one reason:

> God must continually work as the iconoclast. Every idea of Him we form He must in mercy shatter. The most blessed result of prayer would be to rise thinking, 'But I never knew before. I never dreamed.'" (Letters to Malcolm: Chiefly on Prayer)

My experience has been that if we are bringing our disappointments and frustrations to God, He opens us to a new view of Himself. Through the disappointment and perhaps disillusionment, He brings about something new. The French writer Marcel Proust said, "The real voyage of discovery consists not in seeing new landscapes, but in having new eyes."

After being told the cancer was back, I remember so clearly driving down the street after grappling with that sense of disappointment and confusion. I cried out with the same prayer that seemed to arise from my heart over and over, "Okay, I suppose your purposes are still being unfolded in me." I don't have a theology that proclaims God brings suffering in order to teach us lessons or to slow us down, but I do believe that God uses the raw materials of our lives to lead us forward in His purposes ... if we let Him.

God desires willing companions. He won't force us or drag us into a deepening intimacy with Himself but He waits and whispers over and over: "Come, be with Me. I'm here that you would experience a life that is overflowing with abundance."

Are you willing? Are you willing to let Him lead you? Are you willing to release expectations? Are you willing to release disappointment and say, "I trust You, and I believe that You alone are my purpose and reason and hope and life"?

Hey Friends - thank for you following me along on this journey. It means so much. I have experienced His love deeply during these days and you have been a huge part of that.

So, I'll be having surgery on July 27th to try to biopsy the new spot in my chest. They'll have to go in through the ribs on the left side and deflate the left lung to get a sample to biopsy. Many have asked - why don't they just take the growth out and be done with it? Because of the nature of lymphoma (it's a blood cancer), it has to be treated systemically - thus chemotherapy, stem cell/bone marrow transplant, etc.

Thankfully - I won't have anything until after our family vacation. I am so looking forward to these days with my wonderful family. My brother and his wife/kids will be with us as well. Because of the deflated lung, I can't fly for 30 days so even though the plan was to do this surgery ASAP, the surgeon was willing to wait.

Then, if things are confirmed - the real fun will begin ... a few rounds of chemo which will each involve three four-day hospitalizations. This will be followed by the stem cell transplant which will involve at least a one-month hospital stay.

Thanks for your prayers as I try to navigate what this will all mean in terms of schedule and ministry, etc. To a large degree, it seems my primary ministry and service this fall will be toward all the hospital workers, etc. & if this is where the Lord has me, I'm in! We don't always get to choose to whom we minister, and

He is certainly a better "chooser" than me. I trust His wisdom and care during these days.

Friday, July 27   **Surgery Today**

I am heading to the hospital in about 5 minutes and wanted to ask you to pray. I have surgery at noon. Pray that all would go smoothly and that they would be able to get a clear biopsy of the area that is of concern.

Pray that I would be a blessing to all I encounter - sometimes this stuff gets wearying and I can find myself getting a little grouchy. I desire deeply to walk in His grace and provision today.

Saturday, July 28, 2018   **Quick Update - post surgery**

The surgery went well and the surgeon was able to get a good chunk of the mass for biopsy. We still have to get the full pathology report but the initial observation from the surgeon is that they found scar tissue. We don't know what this means and will know more next week when we meet with our oncologist. It could be really good news but we will wait and see (no matter what, we know Him and He is holding it all - good news or bad). Thanks for your prayers yesterday. It helps so much ... this whole journey has put a strain on Jen and me (our relationship) and we were able to process and talk yesterday in the midst of it all. I found myself in a place of deep joy as well - knowing that I am held by Him.

Having had a chest tube inserted as well as a pretty invasive surgery, I am still in the hospital. Pray that I get out today! The pain is pretty constant but they have drugs for that, thankfully.

I will update more when there is more news! Again, thank you for caring about me and being on this journey with me.

Saturday, August 4   **Good News**

Well, my friends ... I had an appointment with my oncologist today and I have some great news. The news is that there is no evidence Hodgkin's lymphoma! I am in remission (those were the words my doctor used). I go back for a PET Scan at the end of September. The biopsy showed no signs of cancer!

So - I'm speechless and teary as it begins to sink in. I am praising God for this particular expression of His grace. It's what I wanted but He didn't have to give this to me. I would be praising Him even now if the news was different. He is so kind and faithful no matter our circumstances. I guess He just thought that this next season will be better for me to free of cancer ... so, I will live into that and praise Him.

I am leading a retreat right now and left this morning during a break for my appointment and only now have had a chance to give this update.

I am grateful for you the way you have supported me during this journey. I realize that I have five years before I am "out of the woods" but I do not feel like I have anything hanging over my head. If I've learned anything during this time, it is to live day by day and trust Him for the day. Right now, I know that I have two months until I might get different news but there is no fear. My life is in His hands. It always has been ... I just have a more acute awareness of this reality and I am grateful.

Much love to you all! Thanks for being willing to pray and join me on this journey!!!!

Sunday, September 23 **Feeling Good**

Hi Everyone ... I can never say it enough. Thank you! Thank you for your prayers and concern over this last year. Twelve months ago, I had just been the doctor to find out why I was feeling so bad - coughing, itching, sleeping all the time. And, they said it might be a sinus infection. It was only 6 more weeks of feeling horrible until a diagnosis.

Today, I feel great. I have lots of energy and I am getting my health back. I'm walking and exercising everyday - hoping that I'll be running a marathon within the year. Almost all my side effects from chemotherapy are gone. I had a good meeting with a cardiologist a few weeks ago and was given a clean bill of health. They were worried that the chemo had done some damage to my heart.

On Wednesday, I have a PET Scan. It will be my first since June when they thought the cancer had returned. I'm not worried about the scan (and not because I think everything will be okay circumstantially but because I know that my life belongs to Him and there is great peace in that!!). So, again, I appreciate your prayers ... for continued good health and that the cancer would stay away. More than, pray that I would continue to live the reality that my life belongs to Him and I will walk into whatever He allows in my life. Truly, my business is to serve Him and my joy is to walk with Him wherever He leads ... His business is to decide where and how and when I walk into certain places. Because of that, cancer is not a fear, more tests are not a fear ... because nothing can separate me from His love. Every circumstance is just a different place and way to know Him more fully and love Him more deeply!

So, grace and peace to you ... I'll let you know when I know more. It could be a week after the scan. We'll see. And, please also know that I'd love to be able to shut down this blog! God willing.

Wednesday, September 26   **PET Scan Results - tough news**
Well, I had the PET Scan this morning and my oncologist called early this afternoon to let me know that the cancer is definitely back. It is in the original spot as well as multiple lymph nodes. She called from the hospital where she was meeting with the radiologist and had already called a doctor at Mayo Clinic who has been consulting on my case. Another surgery (she talked to my surgeon as well) is not advisable for multiple reasons so we will start with 3 rounds of chemo ASAP which will require hospitalization and then a stem cell transplant which will mean at least a month in the hospital.

I am so thankful for your prayers.

I was ready to hear this news but I am still in shock. At the same time, I have a great sense of peace. I've been blogging over the last few weeks about suffering and I have no doubt that our gracious Father has been depositing His truth and His grace deeper into my soul. I feel His presence.

Much love to you all for being on this journey with me. Please pray for Jen and the kids as this is hardest on them.

More soon after we meet with the oncologist next week ...

Friday, October 5   **No News Yet ...**

Just a quick update to tell you there is no new news yet. It appears that several months of intensive treatments lay before me. Likely 9-10 weeks of chemo therapy followed by 3 months of stem cell transplant (with one month of hospitalization followed by isolation at home while the transplant takes).

Much prayer is needed as we seek to rearrange our lives to make space for this experience. We are feeling the ups and downs of processing and receiving this news. Underlying it all is the peace that surpasses all understanding ... as we rest in the glorious truth that our gracious Father leads us into this time and will draw us deeper into His love. The stripping of so much comfort will lead to the reception of His love as truly being enough, actually more than enough.

9

His Plans and His Ways

As I look back on this part of my journey with cancer, I went from being "cancer free" in June to needing a biopsy in July because they found something, back to being "cleared" in August and then back to having cancer in September. It was quite a roller coaster ride but without the exhilaration and excitement. At this point, I was learning how to deal with difficulty but I still found myself reeling because the sand was shifting beneath my feet so quickly.

The uncertainty and waiting can unravel you. Questions about what is going on and what it all might mean can feel quite heavy. Anxiety and fear can take hold.

And at the same time, the challenges to hold things loosely and not identify with circumstances are presented at deepening places in the soul. Again, this is a gift. In a time of difficulty, the eyes of our heart are clearly drawn to focus on what we don't know. And, we can also intentionally focus on what we do know. A great question to ask in time when there is so much we don't know is: *what do I know to be true?*

Simply sitting with that question in prayer is an exercise that can foster deepening intimacy and trust.

When we are not sure what the plan is and what the way forward might be, I think many would say, "I'm looking to God and feeling no peace at all." The truth is that we don't know a lot about the specifics of God's plans for our lives but what we can know is that His plans are good. Perhaps, even more important, we can focus on understanding His *ways* ... how He operates in the world and in the lives of His children.

A great place to start this process is to acknowledge that His ways are not our ways. Isaiah 55:8-9 says: "For my thoughts are not your thoughts, neither are your ways my ways, declares the Lord. For as the heavens are higher than the earth, so are my ways higher than your ways and my thoughts than your thoughts." There is a sense in which we cannot wrap our minds around the way that God works. It is beyond us to comprehend the way He lovingly shapes our lives. What we can know is that He loves us and cares for us. We can trust that He wants the best for us even when we don't know what is best for us. He is present with us. He delights in us.

The conclusion is simple, although not easy to accept: we can trust that no matter the circumstances, He has a plan for using them in good ways. When walking through a storm, this is a reality that we often need to return to over and over again. Like a loose screw on a wobbly chair, this truth of God's ways is like a screwdriver that we use to tighten the screw. In these seasons, wobbly and unstable are par for the course.

And so, in all circumstances, we are able to give thanks because of the way that God is with us in them. (1 Thessalonians 5:18). For clarity, this text doesn't say we necessarily give thanks *for* the circumstance (although that may be a reflection in hindsight) but that we give thanks *in* the circumstance. Why? Because God takes everything and shapes it.

God shapes and forms the circumstances in such a way that our lives would be shaped. And, the nature of that shaping and forming? Put simply, that we would be conformed to His will.

Many discussions of *God's will* fall flat and don't necessarily inspire, especially in time of distress and disappointment. Primarily, this is because we have taken the concept of God's will and interpreted it as a hard, unrelenting standard to which we are required to adapt. If we don't conform, it is suggested, there will be trouble. And, we often see God's will as being the existence of the circumstance itself. There is a bit of mystery in how sovereign God interacts with the events but we do know He doesn't cause evil (James 1:13; 1 Corinthians 14:33).

So, a more accurate understanding of God's will is that His will is His heart. His will speaks of His desire. God's will is a gracious invitation, rather than a harsh standard we have to live up to. He invites us to value what He values.

We have the mind of Christ (1 Cor 2:16) and a new heart in Christ (2 Cor 5:17) and yet, there is the old mind and the old heart. The process of moving further and deeper into living out of this new heart and mind is called sanctification. In 1 Thessalonians 4:3, we are told that this is God's will, His heart for us. And, so we engage in the process of "forgetting what lies behind and straining forward to what lies ahead." (Phil 3:13)

What lies behind? So many things, but in a time of suffering perhaps we are leaving behind our ideas of what life would be like. We leave behind our conceptions of what constitutes the "good life" and our preferences of how God might work in our lives. As we release these things, we can then look toward what lies ahead: the outworking of His plans and His ways.

His plans and His ways are wonderful and good and pure. And so, we can rest into this and trust. In fact, we may be led to a place of saying that *His plans are none of my business; I am along for the ride.* It could sound easy and cliché, but it can be quite a battle to let go of all our conceptions and hold fast to His heart.

In the middle of this summer, I had just left a salaried position at a church which also included sick time and a huge support network. In the prior year, before I was diagnosed, I had prayerfully decided to move into full time ministry in spiritual formation for which I had to raise most of my income the way a missionary might. I had dreamed of what it would be like. I had trusted that God was going to provide. I couldn't wait to move fully into this work that had been on my heart for almost a decade. And then I got the news that

I would be sidelined: not able to travel (which some of the ministry required), not able to fully serve (basically fitting it around treatments and appointments), not able to fundraise. The list could go on but you get the point.

Our family vacation that had been planned for a year was not the best. I found myself angry and anxious. Family was gracious to me, as always, but most of the time I didn't even want to be around me. I thought that I had *my life* back and then I didn't and then I did and then I didn't.

One of the gifts of this kind of suffering is that it caused some things to shake loose: my clinging, my assumptions, my pre-conceived ideas about my life!

My life? When I use those two words, I am saying something that needed attention. My life, my wisdom, my ways. In very basic grammar, we know that the word "my" is a possessive pronoun. I might use the word "my" as a modifier of life to distinguish the specific life to which I am referring and I might use the term to signify possession. For me, I realized that I was possessing this life. In some ways, imperceptible at times, I saw it as mine; *sure, I will use it for God and make it available for His use, but it belongs to me.* In those days, as anxiety and anger rose up, I could see clearly just how much I was clinging to my life. I could feel the reality of my heart: *how dare this present suffering come and try to rob me of my life?*

Meister Eckhardt, the great German mystic of the 13th-14th century wrote so poignantly:

There, where clinging to things ends, is where God begins to be. If a cask is to contain wine, you must first pour out the water. The cask must be bare and empty. Therefore, if you wish to receive divine joy and God, first pour out your clinging to things. Everything that is to receive must and ought to be empty.

As I began to let go of my life, in recognizing to whom I belonged, I began to see new things. I began to appreciate the life I was inhabiting.

I moved from a place of being angry over losing to seeing that something new was emerging. God began to stir a couple of things in my heart. First, if I was going to be in the hospital for extended periods of time, then it was going to become my chapel, my prayer cell. Second, even though I thought I'd be ministering in other places and to other people, it looked like the hospital would be my place of ministry. From there, questions of possibility began to emerge: what new relationships will I form? What ministry will I get to be involved in? In what ways will I grow in prayer and this life with God?

Wednesday, October 17   **Biopsy number 5**

Well, I can still count all the biopsies I've had on one hand! That's good, right? Tomorrow is number five. The surgeon will try to biopsy two lymph nodes by going down the esophagus with a needle and go into my chest. My oncologist explained this as going inside out rather than outside in. Whatever it takes! It will be at 10am on Thursday and I should be home by late afternoon.

It seems that all involved (including second opinions) are not in doubt about the diagnosis (a relapse/recurrence of Hodgkin's Lymphoma) but a biopsy is always prudent. Then, I'll start the intensive chemo next week (I'm still waiting to hear the specifics) followed by the stem cell transplant after 3 rounds of chemo if it all goes well.

Thanks again for your prayers ... pray especially for Jen and the kids. I'm tired of giving these updates but I'm energized knowing that I have a group of people who love and care for me. While I am experiencing so many emotions (up and down), I am anchored in His love and care. It is quite an experience to feel my soul being thrown around in the waves of sadness and doubt but also have the distinct sensation of resting in His goodness because I can feel that anchor for my soul. Hebrews 6 says that we have "hope as a sure and steadfast anchor of the soul because Jesus has gone before us." Grateful and humbled to be experiencing His promises as true in my life.

Saturday, October 20   **Chemo Starts on Tuesday**

The biopsy went well on Thursday. Thanks for all your prayers. Thankfully I ended up under general anesthesia - it was so nice to be asleep while they jabbed my lymph nodes through my trachea. Other than a little fatigue and a scratchy throat for a day, all is good.

I should hear results by Monday or Tuesday but they are still going to start the intensive chemo on Tuesday. They aren't expecting anything other than confirmation from the biopsy so they want to get going quickly and can alter course if they biopsy is surprising in some way. I'll be at the hospital all day Tuesday and then half days (I think) on Wed and Thurs. Then, I get to recover for 21 days - followed by 3 more days of chemo and then a PET Scan. If that goes well and they see a response, I get one more round of 3 days and then the Stem Cell Transplant. That means a month on the hospital.

While the first round of chemo I had last year has a 90% success rate, I was in the 10%. I just had to be special, huh? With this round of treatments, the success/response rate is not so high and this has put us in a place of deepening dependence and living each day with a sense that there are no guarantees. It's actually a great way to live (maybe I've shared that before).

And, my deepest desire in life is to grow in deepening dependence upon Him and His love ... so, He is answering my prayer as I stand on the precipice of going deeper into the wilderness. For that, I am grateful beyond words. That is really all I know and I don't need to know more. That's the reality of dependence, right?

I have this continuing sense that He is guiding this whole journey so that I would be saved, saved from depending on things other than Him. That is pure grace and goodness. In a time of prayer this week, He brought the words of an old hymn to my heart: "I dare not trust the sweetest frame, but wholly lean on Jesus' name." That is my prayer for this season so please pray that more than anything else!

Today, I find myself resting deeply in His love and experiencing peace I can't describe. I like that! I don't like these storms (they aren't good) but I like Him ... a lot.

Much love and peace to you all! And thanks for being a part of this journey with me. I am thankful for the love and connections that He is fostering in this season - another one of His graces.

Tuesday, October 30   **Update after Round 1**

Well - my friends, I'm 1/3 of the way through these current treatments. It was rough to be at the hospital every day last week (with Tuesday being an 11-hour day) but I'm grateful that I don't go back for two weeks. The weekend was brutal - I was in bed all day on Saturday and Sunday, and experienced emotional torment like I never have before. Partially the chemo and partially the circumstance of just feeling horrible, I was feeling emotions that I knew weren't real but there they were.

Questions emerged: "What do I do, Lord?" "Do you love me, Lord?" I could identify that the questions were not my deepest heart, but in grace, He met me in that place and answered my questions with His gentle love and simply invited me to go deeper still with Him.

Today I feel pretty great other than fatigue. This week so far, I seem to feel good in the morning and then midway through the day, I crash. That's ok because it is all a part of the invitation to rest and trust in this season. With my high-achiever personality, finding my identity in His love rather than what I can accomplish in a day is a gracious spiritual discipline that I need. It is being forced on me (of course) but I know it is a loving Father who leading me into it so I am seeking to not resist but receive this gift.

One more thing I'll share ... I am very present to the reality that we are often tempted by just get through tough times rather than receive the gifts that our gracious Father has for us in them. While I grew so much in Him in the last year, I realized that I often thought about "when I get through this." There are never any guarantees in life - except that He is always in the process of drawing me closer to Himself. That is eternal life ... now! That's where I put the attention and intention of my heart.

Saturday, November 17   **One Step Closer to STC**

Well, we're one step closer to the Stem Cell Transplant (STC). I just finished three more days of chemotherapy on Thursday. I've been fairly out of it since and am in bed today just trying to rest. The plan from here is that I will have a PET Scan on Monday Nov 26 to assess how well I've responded to the chemo. The hope is that the cancer is gone and then I'll complete one more round of three days of chemo on Dec 4-6. The goal for me is to be cancer free as I go into the transplant as that will give the best results. If the response has been small but not complete, the STC will still probably happen. If there is no response, we'll reassess with my oncologist on November 30 to determine options.

So, if there has been response, I'll start preparing for the Stem Cell Transplant after I complete the next round of chemo with the hospitalization and transplant likely to start toward the end of December.

Just wanted to keep you all in the loop and thank you for praying. This is more intense than the treatments I did last year and I am definitely feeling weary. Pray for our family as this is definitely a stressor.

I wish that I had more to say but "thank you" feels like enough for today. So - thank you, thank you, thank you.

Wednesday, November 28   **Great News**

Well - my friends, it sounds a little strange to say "Woohoo, I get to have a stem cell transplant!!!" But, that's the news. The PET Scan from Monday revealed that the four cancerous spots have had a complete response to the chemotherapy. So, I will have one more round next week (Tues, Wed, and Thurs) and then I'll recover for a few weeks. The day or two after Christmas, I'll begin all the testing and preparation for the transplant. It will most likely (if everything continues to go smoothly) be the first week of January that I am hospitalized to begin the treatment.

I know it won't be easy but I am encouraged. When I began this latest round of treatments back in October, I began with the Welcome Prayer (written by Thomas Keating):

> *"Welcome, welcome, welcome. I welcome everything that comes to me in this moment because I know it is for my healing. I welcome all thoughts, feelings, emotions, persons, situations and conditions. I let go of my demand for security. I let go of my hunger for approval. I let go of my insistence on control. I let go of my blind desire to change any situation, condition, person, or myself. I open to the love and presence of God and the healing action and grace within."*

So, this is part of my prayer and spiritual practice during these days ... welcoming whatever comes my way as a part of my "healing" - of course, this prayer is talking about spiritual healing which is the essence of everything anyway. All that I am going through is part of this healing ... so, I welcome that and

I am also choosing to see the difficult days that are coming with the transplant as a part of physical healing as well! So - I can receive it with joy because it is the best option for physical healing. I leave the results in God's hands with the knowledge that He is doing a deeper work in me than I could ever imagine. I read the following in a book that I am devouring in this season, *The Solace of Fierce Landscapes*, "wilderness holds answers to more questions than we yet know how to ask." I am thankful that He is leading me into these difficult places where layers of sin and self-sufficiency (of which I couldn't have even been aware) are being peeled back.

As always, thanks for your prayer and love and support. The notes, the texts, the phone calls - all mean so much! Grace and Peace as you enter this advent season - a season of waiting and expectancy ... a gracious gift to get to remember that our souls long for what only Christ brings.

Friday, December 7 **Another Week of Chemo Finished!**
The other day at church, someone didn't recognize me. All my hair is now gone and the eye brows aren't far behind. I may not have any hair but if you see me, I hope you can see the joy in my eyes as I continue to receive the gifts of this season: the gifts of being unraveled, being stripped down! I know they don't sound like gifts but they are ... to have only Him to which I cling ... that's the good stuff of life!

Yesterday, I finished my final round of "preparatory" chemo as we continue to march toward the stem cell transplant. Thank you for your prayers this week - I have felt His strength in the midst of getting chemicals pumped into my body.

Here is a brief overview of the schedule:
Everything starts on December 27-28: medical tests and education classes all day.
January 4-11 - Stem Cell Collection (outpatient)
January 15-22 - Chemo (24/7) (inpatient)
January 23 - Stem Cell Transplant (inpatient)
January 24-Feb 7 - recover at the hospital

I know I say it every time but I don't feel I can ever say it enough: thank you for your prayers and support. It really does make a difference. I know that our Father is at work as we hold one another up. And know that I am praying for you!

Friday, December 28　　　　　　**The Process has Started**
Yesterday I was at the hospital from 7:45-5:00 with tests/classes, etc. In a few minutes, I go in for a Bone Marrow Biopsy followed by heart tests and more classes. This whole process will be as intense as I thought, maybe more so. I received a huge binder with all the transplant information as well as all the instructions for how the collection of my stems will work.
For those who are confused - and it is a lot to hold together as far as info ... I am having what has usually been called a Bone Marrow Transplant — also called Stem Cell Transplant. They spend 4 days collecting stem cells from me, they freeze the cells,

I have 7 days of high dose chemo therapy to reset my system, and then the transplant. It will then take at least 100 days for me to get back to baseline "normal." I have a chemotherapy port but will also have a special line put in my neck

10

Deeper into the Wilderness of Love

As I stood on the precipice of three days of having stems cells extracted, I remember it feeling quite momentous. In the days leading up the extraction, I went to the stem cell unit at the hospital and got daily injections to stimulate cell production. I started to get a sense of what was coming as I saw people hooked up to machines. The Lord was leading me into a deeper place than I had been and I had been through a few things. I didn't know all that the coming days would hold but it was clear to me that they would be a form of wilderness.

Wilderness.

Desert.

Our gracious God will lead us through seasons of wilderness. He will take us into the desert. For many, grace and desert appear to be contradictory. The desert can make us feel quite vulnerable and that was certainly my experience. As Jesus went in the desert as described in Mark 1, he was confronted with wild animals as well as temptation. The desert is a risky, vulnerable space. However, in *Soul Making*, Alan Jones makes the observation: "From the point of view of the believer, the purpose of emptiness and desolation is to prepare us for joy and ground us in hope. Unless joy and hope are the goal, the desert becomes a playground for masochists." Perhaps, even deeper is the idea that the wilderness is a place where we experience pure, unmediated love and presence. While we may initially consider a wilderness season as a place of loss and dryness and danger, we soon begin to realize that it is a place of encounter. When all the usual distractions like happiness and health are taken away, we are left bare.

In Matthew 4, we learn that the Holy Spirit led (or, more literally, the Greek word could be translated as "pushed") Jesus into the wilderness. It was a place of danger and loneliness and temptation. The temptations were specifically centered around three things which are the pattern we find in the Garden of Eden in Genesis 3 and also described in 1 John 2. Henri Nouwen describes these temptations as rooting our identity in what we have, what we do, and what others think of us.

We experience these same temptations. The encouragement to turn stones into bread was a temptation toward power, control, and cultivating our own sense of strength through what we do. The whisper of the enemy to jump off the temple and be saved by angels was a temptation to be spectacular, to create a brand, to be seen by others. Finally, Jesus is confronted with the temptation to bow to the devil and have all "these things" which mirrors our own temptations to possess and to find security through what we have.

Each of these temptations are a pattern that appeals to the core of who we are as humans. We have a need for strength, significance, and security. God created us as dependent beings and we are tempted over and over to be independent – to create a life in our own power and strength. The invitation of the desert is to confront these temptations head on, to see them for what they are. The gift of the wilderness is that all the illusions are taken away. When we are lying in a hospital bed unable to do much more than sit up when the nurse comes in to give medication, we are under no illusions. These times can lead us into despair, anger, or denial; and it also possible to move into a place of glad surrender.

When we can't pick up the familiar instruments we've used our whole lives to navigate difficult things, the realities become quite stark. We can sink into despair and denial, or we can see our lives for what they are: in the hands of an infinite, loving, merciful, present God who waits to be gracious to us. Pedro Arrupe, a Jesuit priest, shared:

> More than ever, I find myself in the hands of God. This is what I wanted all my life from my youth. But now there is a difference; the initiative is entirely with God. It is indeed a profound experience to know and feel myself so totally in God's hands.

In Isaiah 30, God challenges His people: "In returning and rest you shall be saved; in quietness and in trust shall be your strength." As we enter into those postures, we are laying down our devices, our strategies. The text in Isaiah goes on to say: "But you were unwilling, and you said, 'No! We will flee upon horses.'" In the ancient world, horses were a symbol of power and strength and here the people are responding to God by saying, *we've got this.* And then God responds with grace: "Therefore the Lord waits to be gracious to you, and therefore he exalts himself to show mercy to you. For the Lord is a God of justice; blessed are all those who wait for him." So, God invites, He offers, He waits. He never forces us to trust and rest in Him but He always meets us in the events of our lives and invites.

A time of serious illness can be a gift beyond anything we've experienced. While it is theoretically possible that I could have "learned" what I did during these days outside of suffering, I do not believe it would have been much more than "head" knowledge. Information is a good thing, but transformation in the presence of God is everything.

In this part of my journey, I could feel the Spirit leading me forward or, as in Matthew 4, pushing me. I was fully aware that God could have (in His power) stopped the cancer that had been growing in my body but He did not. I was also aware that it wasn't that He couldn't but He wouldn't. What this left me with was a sense that He must be up to something, He must be doing something that is too beautiful for me to imagine.

In Job 42:3 in the Hebrew Scriptures, we read: "'Who is this that hides counsel without knowledge?' Therefore, I have uttered what I did not understand, things too wonderful for me, which I did not know." In Psalm 139:6, David talks about the ways of God and proclaims, "Such knowledge is too wonderful for me; it is high, I cannot attain it." Rather than perceive things that cannot be fully understood as stumbling blocks, the writers of the Scriptures routinely saw them rooted in wonder. However, arriving at such a place is never portrayed as being without struggle. As pain and confusion and doubt are brought to God, there is an opportunity for each to be transformed into wonder.

And, that is where the Lord was leading me at this point, wondering: *God, what are you up to? God, what do you have up your sleeve? What will you be leading me into?* Wonder is a choice and it often emerges from struggle.

In Genesis 28, Jacob had a dream in which he saw a ladder which extended from the earth into heaven. On the ladder were angels that are described as ascending and descending. The angels represent God's activity in Jacob's life, and God tells Jacob, "I am with you and will keep you wherever you go." Jacob's response is to say, "Surely the Lord is in this place, and I did not know it." It is a response of wonder.

When we live in the awareness of God's presence and activity in our lives, it leads us to wonder ... a joyful, expectant sense of wonder ... noticing the ways He is loving us.

Tuesday, January 8   **Stem Cell Collection Begins Today**

A quick note to ask specifically for prayer this week. Please pray today and through the end of the week that the stem cell collection goes well. I had a catheter inserted into my neck yesterday and it has three lines from which stem cells will be collected from my blood. If the thought of having a line coming out of one's neck sounds weird, it is! It feels so strange. However, I'll have it taken out as soon as they get enough stem cells. Yesterday was painful and uncomfortable, and this morning as I wake up - I am feeling rested and ready. Several of my blood counts weren't high enough yesterday so they had to do some extra infusions and injections to get me ready.

I am humbled by your prayers and love for me in these days. I feel His strength and His joy so deeply and I have no doubt that you are a part of that. A word that I've been pondering quite a bit lately is "abide" which essentially means to stay put, to remain. (John 15) In fearful times, it is easy to "take off" and go somewhere else - to let my mind and heart enter into despair or even false hope. I desire so deeply to stay in place - to be present to Him in all that is going on. He is not leading me through all these things except for love - loving Him more intimately and loving others more intensely. I don't want to run from love but to stay and abide. That's really my biggest prayer but please pray for the other "stuff" too!!

Wednesday, January 9   **A Twist and a Turn**

Just when I thought we were starting the transplant process; the plug has been pulled. The plan is scrapped for now. I started collection of the stem cells on Tuesday and it didn't go well.

I didn't produce very many stem cells. And, when analyzed - the cells weren't considered viable. Some of my blood counts just aren't right. We have a team of doctors who are working with us on this part of the process and they all seem to be stumped as to why it didn't work and why my blood counts/levels are where they are. Now, it seems we might be back to the drawing board. Honestly, we just don't know a lot right now. We have an appointment with our primary oncologist next Tuesday when we will hopefully learn more about treatments options going forward.

So, while the last day has been taxing emotionally and mentally and physically, we have felt so grounded spiritually. Thanks for the role you are playing in that. Please continue to pray for us as we are in a state of waiting and uncertainty.

There have been tears and questions in the midst of it all, and right now I can say that I am just wondering what the Lord has next in this journey. It seems with every disappointment and set back comes a deeply purifying perspective on life and what it means to abide in His love. Feeling some of that purifying today and I just want to keep living there. There are so many layers to the illusion of control that we think we have over life and so many layers to what it means to live a life surrendered to Him - relinquishing and releasing that control. I am seeing more of that releasing today and I am grateful.

Much to love to you all ... as always, thanks for journeying along. Will let you know when we know more and until then, thanks for your prayers for wisdom for the doctors and abiding in His love for us.

Wednesday, January 16   **Tough News to Share**

We now know why the stem cell transplant didn't work. In addition to Hodgkin's Lymphoma, I now have Leukemia. If you can imagine the shock of hearing the news that you have cancer, imagine what it might be like to hear that you have cancer when you already have cancer! Ahhh. We are still in shock, trying to process it all.

After the stem cell transplant had to be cancelled last week, they sent some of my bone marrow for further testing. It came back showing that I have a couple of chromosomal abnormalities which suggest Acute Myeloid Leukemia. Most likely, I developed the leukemia as a result of the chemotherapy I had last year. What is strange (to the doctors, anyway) is that I developed leukemia so quickly. Secondary cancers are not unheard of but usually not like this because I'll now be battling both cancers. The plan right now is to have a bone marrow biopsy on Monday to double check what they saw in the previous biopsy. I have also been experiencing a lot of bone pain in my neck and shoulder so they are doing X-rays and MRIs on these areas to rule out some things as well. From there (if it is confirmed), I would quickly be admitted to the hospital for a month of chemo therapy to put the leukemia in remission. If they are able to do that and the Hodgkin's is still at bay, then they will attempt another stem cell transplant but this time with a donor because my existing bone marrow and stem cells just won't work.

So, pray for this whole process and for physical healing. The doctor used the words "concerned" and "concerning" several times so this is a big deal. Jenifer just says that I like to be "special" and do things that are unexpected (she says this tongue in cheek, of course). I say that Lord is good and He is doing things beyond what I can understand.

As always, pray that we would be able to be present to Him each day and not squander the gifts of this season. Honestly, it is hard to see the gifts or goodness when I look at the big picture but everyday there is gift after gift. I think I understand more deeply why Jesus said, "Therefore do not be anxious about tomorrow, for tomorrow will be anxious for itself. Sufficient for the day is its own trouble." Trouble can only be encountered with God one day at a time. I came across this recently and spoke deeply to me: "Difficulties should not depress or divert us. The cause that has gripped us is so great that the small weaknesses of individuals cannot destroy it. Therefore, I ask you only one thing: do not be so worried about yourself. Free yourself from all your plans and aims. They occupy you far too much. Surrender yourself to the sun, the rain, and the wind, as do the flowers and the birds. Surrender yourself to God. Wish for nothing but one thing: that his will be done, that his kingdom come, and that his nature be revealed. Then all will be well." (Eberhard Arnold)

In some ways, I feel like all the clichés of the faith have dropped away and now the Lord is going to walk me through things which clichés can't even pretend to address. For that I am grateful. Pray for Jen and the kids ... this is not easy for them ... and they are my main concern these days!

11

What to Do When We Don't Know What to Do

The extraction of my stem cells occurred in a unit just down that hall from where Jenifer works as a nurse. She happened to be working the day I got the news that the stem cells weren't viable. When I initially heard from the pathologist, I asked if I could walk down the hall and bring my wife back so we could receive the news together. As I walked down the hallway and approached the desk where she sat, she immediately saw the look on my face and asked, "What's wrong?" I burst into tears, and then we walked back down the hallway together.

There are those days when it feels like we just need to take a deep breath and figure out how to regroup. And then, there are days like this when it is hard to even see how are the pieces could ever be picked up and reassembled. Taking a deep breath sounds great but it feels like all the breath has been knocked out of us. We have no idea how to get our bearings. We don't know what to do. So, what do we do when we don't know what to do?

As simple as it may sound, pray. Seek God in the midst of it all.

But not the sweet, gentle kind of prayer that we might be used to. When you are left broken and heart broken, a prayer of lament is invited. It is invited by God and modeled in the prayer book of the Scriptures, the Psalms, where approximately two thirds of the collection of prayers are lament. And, a whole book of the Bible, Lamentations, is a long lament. A prayer of lament is a cry to God, asking questions and making statements that arise from the depths of our being. For example: "my soul is bereft of peace; I have forgotten what happiness is." (Lamentations 3:17)

It is not uncommon when we are struggling deeply to have people share things about God that are true but not appropriate for the moment. There are lots of beautiful things we could say about God and His character, but they are things that would sound platitudinous at best or demeaning at worst. It is hard when we're feeling lost and it seems like God isn't present the way we'd expected. In the midst of doubt and fear and hurt and confusion, the reality that God exists and that we can seek Him can become a sufficient place for us, and the journey to that place isn't a straight line. God desires for us to draw near to Him even if it means pounding on His chest, demanding answers, and telling Him we're not sure if we trust His goodness. Because God loves us and nothing can ever change that, He is present with us, holding our lament like treasures because lament is proof that desire is alive. Doubt is proof that belief is a value in our lives. Hurt means that we have a heart.

As we intentionally move into lament and the gravity of what we are experiencing with God, it can open us to experiencing the God who is the lover of our souls. Rather than relying on platitudes, lament lead us into an experience of God's presence and active love in our lives. I noticed that as I expressed my fears, doubts, and hurts in His presence, I was given new eyes to see the world around me. It is hard to explain but I felt a clarity and simplicity of vision when all I was able to let go of it all through lament.

Lament can lead us into deep places of clarity as we entrust all that we are to God. Whatever emotions arise, however negative they may seem, each of them is an opportunity to notice with God.

Lament can feel a bit counterintuitive. We might think that lament, prayers of doubt or anger or uncertainty or frustration, would drive us away from God. Instinctively, we might be tempted to hide such things. However, the reality is that we are driven closer to the heart of God. How is this true?

First, lament is prayer, communicating with God. Communication deepens relationships. It is the expression of desire. Even if it is "negative" communication, it forges connection. It leads us to abiding and remaining.

Second, lament brings all of what we are experiencing in the presence of God, and if we are open there is a possibility for doubt to move toward faith, for anger to shift toward trust, for uncertainty to reorient toward relationship.

Midway through my first round of chemotherapy, I went through a stretch of time in which I couldn't sleep. I was experiencing significant pain which, when mixed with a lot of steroids infused during chemo, kept me up at night. My mind would race and I found myself crying out to God. Really crying out, I felt desperate. During these times, I found music to be a gift. There were songs that gave words to my experience and allowed me to express things that I wasn't in a state to fully formulate. A song called, "Lord, I Need You," became a mantra as I sang it quietly over and over again. I needed that mantra because I didn't have words of my own. The lyrics proclaimed "every hour I need You, my one defense, my righteousness, O God how I need You." There were times when it was a deep lament. I needed Him but it often felt like the words were just floating into the universe. I kept singing, I kept crying out, and I kept trusting even though I wasn't necessarily finding physical relief.

What I did find over and over was a frame for what I was experiencing. Lament was that frame. A frame that held everything, even if unresolved. A frame that made it clear that my life was in God and in His hands. In those days when the hopelessness of sleeplessness was so present, through crying out to God I was able to release my need to know specific answers and settle in to knowing that He was holding it all.

In these days of finding out that I had developed a new cancer in the midst of cancer treatment, prayers of lament helped me rest. The circumstances were beyond confusing and disheartening, but I was able to rest as practicing lament helped me put things in a frame and feel that He was holding me.

Tuesday, January 22   **Update/In Hospital**

Hey friends - just thought I'd send a quick update. I had blood tests and a bone marrow biopsy on Monday and almost as soon as I got home - the doc called and said they wanted to admit me to the hospital. Apparently, the biopsy did indeed show that I have Acute Myeloid Leukemia and because it is a quickly moving cancer - they want to start treatment immediately.

So - here we go. It was a rough day as there was so much to take in so quickly. I am now working with a leukemia specialist who will also lead me into a stem cell transplant.

I will be here at least 28 days. If all goes well, then I'll get about 2 weeks off and the start the transplant. This transplant will be different because it will require a donor and will likely mean I'm out of commission much longer than the other transplant. I will share more details as I have them but I wanted to get some basics to you so you know how to pray. Pray that I am stabilized so I can receive treatment – I have had a very high fever all night. Pray that the chemo treatments go well and that my body is responsive. Of course, I am so overwhelmed by your love and generosity in prayer.

I am doing well and once I got in my room last night I very much felt the Lord's presence and plan in all of this. What grace from our father!!! I know that there are purposes for these next 28 days for me physically and I also have this deep sense that there are purposes that the Lord has for us together.

P.S. Update on Wednesday: we have not started chemo yet as
we have run into some complications: a blood clot in my chemo
port (so they are removing this afternoon), some decrease in
heart function, and probably some other stuff that I can't
remember because I am so tired!!

*Note: The following blog posts are from Jenifer. You'll see why I wasn't
able to post anything myself for about a month.*

Monday, January 28   **Guest Post from Jenifer**
Hi friends - this is Jenifer. I wanted to update you all on how
Ted is doing.

He was able to start chemo last Wednesday and will finish
chemo tomorrow morning. So far, he is tolerating chemo fairly
well with no unusual side effects. However, the usual side effects
are no fun as they are mostly gastrointestinal side effects. Please
pray the side effects are minimized. On a positive note, the
chemo is doing its job and wiping out all of his blood counts
and presumably the leukemia too. Because all his blood counts
are low (hemoglobin, white blood cells, platelets, potassium,
and magnesium) he has gotten several blood and platelet
transfusions, as well as potassium and magnesium infusions. He
is still having frequent fevers, which is not uncommon with
leukemia. But, because his body cannot fight off infection right
now they monitor his temperature very closely as well as any
other signs of infection. He is also on antibiotics because he
came into the hospital with a virus and they want to prevent any
further infection.

Any further infection could potentially be very dangerous for Ted. Because of this we are limiting visitors. If you would like to visit Ted in the hospital, please contact me and I will let you know if he is feeling up for a visit. I'm sure you can imagine how difficult it is for Ted to not be around people! I asked him today if he felt lonely or isolated. He said that he feels too terrible to feel lonely or isolated. So, that is how miserable he is feeling today. If you would like to send him a card or note of encouragement, I know he would love it.

It is difficult to see him feeling so miserable and to feel helpless to help him feel better. Trey and Claire are doing okay. It is hard for them to see Ted feeling weak, miserable, and not his usual self. I am hanging in there too. Just trying to take one day at a time. We all appreciate your thoughts and prayers and feel your love.

Many of you have asked how you can help. First and foremost, we appreciate you praying for us all. Especially for Ted's healing. We know this is a long road and we know we need the Lord's strength, direction, and love to sustain and protect us. If you feel led to help in other ways, gift cards are very helpful. We appreciate all the ways you all are loving and caring for all of us. Thank you!

Wednesday, February 6   **Update on Ted**

Last night as the sun was setting, I was reminded that even in the midst of the storms of life God can create beauty. Yesterday as I was driving up to the hospital to visit Ted, there was a rainbow in the sky over the Mayo Clinic. Another reminder of God's beauty and hope. And the cards, notes, gifts, emails, and texts we are receiving daily from all of you are yet another reminder of the beauty of the love, care, and kindness of the community of people supporting us through this. Thank you for being instruments of God. We are trusting Him with each day and what it brings and experiencing the beauty of His presence and peace.

Ted finished chemo last Tuesday and has been dealing with the effects of that. He is feeling a little better each day. It will take a couple of weeks for his body to recover from the chemo and once his blood counts are back up, he will get to go home. Yesterday he had another lumbar puncture and bone marrow biopsy. We have not received the results of the bone marrow biopsy yet, but our prayer has been for no abnormal cells to be in the biopsy. If they do continue to see abnormal cells in the bone marrow, he will most likely have more chemo. We will let you know the results when we find out. Thank you for journeying with us. We are so grateful for your prayers and support.

Friday, February 8   **Thank you!**

Ted's room is filled with all the cards and notes you all have sent. They are an encouraging reminder of everyone praying for

him. Thank you does not adequately express how thankful we
are for your encouragement, support, and prayers. We are so
grateful for your love.

We have some good news to share- The bone marrow biopsy
that Ted had on Tuesday did not show any abnormal
cells/cancer. Yay! And, the lumbar puncture he had on Tuesday
and the one done today did not show any abnormal
cells/cancer. So, the chemo is working and he should not have
to have any more chemo at this time. Yay! And, today we heard
that they have found a stem cell donor that is a 100% match for
Ted. Yay! Yay!

So, the plan is for him to keep recovering from chemo, increase
his blood counts, and stay well. He should be able to go home
in about 10 days. Then he will continue to recover at home for
two weeks and will be admitted to the hospital again in March
for the stem cell transplant. We know God is with us through
this. Thank you for being with us too.

Tuesday, February 19   **28 Days and Counting!**
Hi friends! Today is Ted's 28th day since starting chemo. We
are still waiting for his blood counts to come back up, mainly
his white blood cells. Today the oncologist told us that since
Ted received a high dose of chemo, we might not see an
increase until day 32. So, we wait.

For the last several days Ted has been experiencing shortness of
breath and is now wearing oxygen. This is partly due to the fact

that he has developed a lung infection, but also because his heart function has decreased. Decreased heart function is one of the potential side effects/complications of chemo. Today a cardiologist saw Ted and believes the decreased heart function will improve with medication and time.

We all have our moments of weariness but continue to focus on taking one day at a time. We are buoyed by your encouraging messages, earnest prayers, thoughtful notes, and kind gifts - they are reminders of God's love and care for us all through this. The other evening Ted and I sat on his bed recounting Matthew 6:26-34 to each other:

> Look at the birds of the air; they neither sow nor reap nor gather into barns, and yet your Heavenly Father feeds them. Are you not of more value than they? ... Therefore, do not be anxious about tomorrow, for tomorrow will be anxious for itself. Sufficient for the day is its own trouble.

Thursday, February 21 **Do not be anxious about tomorrow**
My previous update on Ted, two days ago, ended with Matthew 6:26-34. At the time we did not know what "tomorrow" would bring, but we were prepared. Yesterday Ted's breathing became much more labored and his heart was weak. The team of doctors decided to transfer him to the ICU to give him stronger intravenous medications and monitor him more closely. This morning he is feeling better and his vital signs and blood tests are improving. He will probably be in the ICU for at least another day while the medical team adjusts his medication regimen to optimize his heart function and breathing.

It was a little scary, even for a nurse (especially for a nurse!), to hear your husband is being transferred to the ICU. However, I am so thankful for the excellent care he is receiving from everyone. I knew I worked at one of the best hospitals in the country, but I have a new appreciation for what that means. It is certainly different being on the receiving end. I am thankful for the Mayo Clinic. And, I am thankful and grateful for all of you - our friends and family - that are caring for us, praying for us, and loving us each day and each "tomorrow".

Monday, February 25   **Things are looking up!**
Ted was transferred out of the ICU on Saturday night and moved *up* to the Progressive Care Unit (the unit I work on!). He is feeling better and breathing much better. He is off the IV heart and blood pressure medications and off oxygen. The doctors are adjusting his medications to determine the right regimen for him. Also, today Ted's white blood cell count is *up* slightly. This is the first increase since he had chemo over four weeks ago. He will probably be moving back to an oncology unit today since his heart problem is more under control and we are back to focusing on wiping out the leukemia.

Please pray that Ted's white blood cell count keeps increasing so that he can go home soon for a couple of weeks before the stem cell transplant. Thank you for your continued encouragement, support, and prayers.

12

Being Held by God

When I was a junior in high school, we had a unit in English literature called *Appearance vs. Reality*. I'll never forget the way it shaped my 17-year-old brain to remember that there is a way that things often appear that doesn't match reality.

When we deal with difficult, perhaps even life-threatening, circumstances appearances can tell us one thing, yet there is always a deeper reality at work. The apostle Paul says it so well in 2 Corinthians 4:16-18:

> So, we do not lose heart. Though our outer self is wasting away, our inner self is being renewed day by day. For this light momentary affliction is preparing for us an eternal weight of glory beyond all comparison, as we look not to the things that are seen but to the things that are unseen. For the things that are seen are transient, but the things that are unseen are eternal.

No matter how dark the sky, no matter how strong the winds, no matter how hopeless things seem to be, there is something deeper and more profound. By God's grace, we get tastes of this reality and it gives us hope.

There is a hope that that we can access quite freely through our mind that may make its way to our heart. And, then there is a hope that comes from lived experience that is experienced in the heart and makes its way to our mind.

When I was laying in the ICU for several days, I had tubes connected to every opening in my body (I'll let you do the math on that one). There was part of me that knew the circumstances weren't great when I was rushed from my "regular" hospital room the ICU very quickly. I had an extra line put into my jugular vein and an arterial line into my arm. This was in addition to the lines already placed in my chest for other treatments. Then, when the director of the ICU department, the director of the cardiac department, the ICU chaplain, and the chaplain from another floor came to see me, there was a sense that things were dicey. And, at the same time, I experienced something that is not easy to describe.

As I laid in that ICU bed, I had a growing awareness that God was holding my life. It might not have been quite a physical sensation but it was close. I sensed God's nearness and deep sense of peace that He was with me and loving me when I wasn't able to do much at all. I couldn't do much in terms of praying, I couldn't even think very clearly. I could just hear the constant pulse of machines and the beeping of devices that were keeping me alive.

In moments like these, it is indeed the Spirit who prays in us. Romans 8:26-27 describes it like this:

> Likewise the Spirit helps us in our weakness. For we do not know what to pray for as we ought, but the Spirit himself intercedes for us with groanings too deep for words. And he who searches hearts knows what is the mind of the Spirit, because the Spirit intercedes for the saints according to the will of God.

The idea is that when we are too weak to form words or prayer, the Spirit does our praying for us. And not only that, consider this passage from Hebrews 7:25, "Consequently, he (Jesus) is able to save to the uttermost those who draw near to God through him, since he always lives to make intercession for them."

The Father, Son, and Holy Spirit holding our lives in love and having a conversation about us constantly. It is in this sense that the Triune God holds our lives. Here's the beauty of this reality: in many ways, we are always too weak to pray, always too limited in our perspective to know how to pray, always too self-absorbed to not make it about us, and even in all that, the Spirit holds our lives in conversation with the Son and the Father.

Lying in that ICU I experienced this reality as I released all control. In many ways, I had no other choice. My body was weak, my mind was foggy, and my will was weary but my spirit was able to release and surrender. To be clear, I wasn't necessarily trying to surrender but it was graciously laid upon me. Like Jesus being "pushed" in the wilderness, I had a sense that I was pushed into this place of surrender.

To be sure, it was the most terrible time of my life. And, it was one of the most amazing moments of my life. Even though it looked like my body was wasting away, my inner life was being renewed as I was growing into deepening intimacy with God.

As I've pondered my own death over the last few years and even in this experience, I've reflected on the idea that this might be what the dying process is like for one who knows Christ. No fighting but a glad surrender and releasing as we are welcomed into the eternal realm.

Could this be why the pattern of Scripture and the words of Jesus in the Gospel use death imagery over and over again to talk about our spiritual journey? "Whoever finds his life will lose it, and whoever loses his life for my sake will find it." (Matthew 10:39) "If anyone would come after me, let him deny himself and take up his cross and follow me. For whoever would save his life will lose it, but whoever loses his life for my sake will find it." (Matthew 16:24-25)

As we cling and hold on tight, we are scarcely aware that God is holding our lives. And, as when we release and lose all those things we've relied upon to make us feel safe and secure, we are finally in a place where we live in intense awareness of His hold on our lives. That realized sense of awareness is what Jesus means by "find our life." The paradox is beautifully laid out by Jesus. Our clinging and holding tight actually disintegrate life, and releasing and losing integrates our life with His. How so?

When we come to know Christ, the reality is that we are then "hidden with Christ in God." (Colossians 3:3) Galatians 4:5 tells us that we have "received adoption as sons." We are connected, we are in. However, this reality might not be integrated into our lives. We might not be experiencing that connection. This is the invitation.

To develop this further, this is certainly what Jesus meant in John 15 when He discussed the idea of "abiding."

> "I am the true vine, and my Father is the vinedresser. Every branch in me that does not bear fruit he takes away, and every branch that does bear fruit he prunes, that it may bear more fruit." (vv. 1-2)

It is established that Jesus is speaking to those who are branches, those who have a connection. The point, in this analogy, is to bear fruit. The fruit is described later in John 15 love, joy, peace, and hope. To be clear, much like the fruit of the Spirit discussed in Galatians 5, fruit is not something we produce but something that grows as a response to relationship.

As we "abide" and experience active connection, there is fruit. If the branch is not bearing fruit, the Father, the vinedresser, will "take away" that branch. "Take away" is an unfortunate translation because the Greek verb *airo* could be better translated as "lift up." It was a common process in viticulture to lift up or prop up branches that struggle.

Clearly, God the Father gets involved in the process of fruit being borne in our lives. He will shift and move in the events of our lives so that we will live into the depths of our connection with Him.

Jesus' encouragement is to abide, to remain, to stay. This abiding life requires an abandon and surrender to the reality that God is present more than we could ever imagine, He is loving us more than we could comprehend. He is at work in us more than we ever could ask for.

When we suffer, we lose so much and what we end up being left with is: His love and presence. That is all that remains. That is what abides. And, it is more than sufficient.

Tuesday, March 5   **I'm Home**

After 44 days, I am home. My counts came up and it was time to come home. Other than fatigue, I feel really well. Thanks to my more than amazing wife, Jen, for keeping you all updated so well.

Here's what I know right now: I had a bone marrow biopsy last Friday which showed no signs of leukemia! The sixth (and final) lumbar puncture showed no signs of leukemia. So, the next step is the stem cell transplant. It (as you may remember) will involve at least a 28 day stay in the hospital and will likely happen 3-4 weeks from now. I need that time to recover - I lost a lot of weight and strength in these last weeks.

I had been praying that I would be home for Ash Wednesday and what a gift from the Father (came home the day before). The things I've experienced in these last six weeks are hard to put in words except to say that I felt held by the Father in ways I never have and in ways that are too wonderful for words. You may remember me quoting an ancient church Father who said, "Go to you cell and your cell will teach you everything." Being in that small space (in some ways) felt like a monastic experience but there was always a stream of doctors and nurses coming in and out and I was constantly confronted with the questions: how can I show hospitality? How can I love these people? Love is so central and so purifying and I felt that deeply. I learned that I don't need to do anything or accomplish anything to be loved ... I could go on.

Thank you to all who have given to us, prayed for us, landscaped our yard, visited, sent cards (several people at the hospital commented that they'd never seen so many cards), etc. You guys are amazing! Thank you. Please keep praying that in these next weeks at home I am able to gain back some strength, stay well (I still have low counts), and keep my eyes on the Father.

Saturday, March 9   **Next Steps**

As always, we are so honored and grateful that you walk with us during these challenging days! We met with my oncologist yesterday and got a bit of a game plan for the next steps:

1. I need to get strong enough to go into the stem cell transplant. This relates primarily to my heart. For those who know heart stuff, my Ejection Fraction got down to 33% from a normal in the 50s. That number needs to be above 40%. All in all - pray for a strengthened heart. I have an echocardiogram on March 18 as well as blood tests.

2. I have another bone marrow biopsy on March 20 to see if I continue to be free of the leukemia and will have a PET Scan somewhere in there to see about the Hodgkin's lymphoma (my original diagnosis).

3. The week after that (March 25 and following) - I'll have daily chemo treatments as a "bridge" to transplant. If the biopsy shows anything, I might have additional chemo.

4. Aside from other tests, etc. - it looks like I'll start the transplant process at the end of April/first of May. It will mean about a month (maybe less) in the hospital.

Thanks for caring about all this stuff! It is good to be home! I love these people and love that they don't have to trek over to a hospital to see me every day. I find myself getting stronger every day and only took one nap yesterday! Wearing a mask when I go outside, I am now walking a bit each day - .75 miles yesterday. For those who know I used to run marathons, this number is small but it feels big and I am thankful for HIS healing touch and presence in all of this.

I am doing so well and seeing God loving me and drawing me to His heart. As I've shared before, I feel so drawn to love well. I want to live but not so that I can accomplish anything or achieve but that I might love. To be sure, if my prayer is to live - it's a prayer to love because THAT is the essence of life ... everything else is just noise (1 Corinthians 13).

Love you all. You are my heroes.

Tuesday, March 26   **Update and New Dates**
Over the last week, we have received some great news. First, my heart function test revealed that my heart is back in the normal range. (not just good enough to enter transplant but in the normal range) Second, the bone marrow biopsy showed no evidence of leukemia and is actually showing signs of healthy production of cells.

So, when we met with the oncologist yesterday, she said, "You are ready to go." Initially, I was going to have chemotherapy all week as a "bridge" to transplant while my body got stronger but she said, "let's not wait." So, I will be admitted to the hospital on April 4 with the transplant happening on April 10. Initially, we thought we'd have to wait until the end of April or first of May.

When admitted, I will have chemotherapy for 6 days to kill off as much of my present bone marrow as possible. Then, on day 7, I will receive the stem cells from the donor. This will take about 6 hours. My transplant coordinator is working with the Donor Center right now to determine if the donor (who is in Germany) will be ready to donate on the 8th so the stem cells can be flown here by the 10th. I'll then be in the hospital for a few more weeks as the transplant takes hold. This will be followed by being at home with a 24/7 caregiver (for me, I have the best nurse in the world at the helm). And then, up to a year of recovery - there are a lot of potential challenges in this process.

Those are the facts. That is the plan. We hold it all loosely, knowing that things can change and trusting that HE is in charge of it all ultimately.

My request for prayer in all of this is two-fold. First, for healing, I do want this treatment to work! Second, for continued growth in His love - because it's the only reason to live anyway, whether

for another year or another 25. I've come across two
quotes recently that spoke deeply to me ...

> *"Your task is not to seek love, but merely to find all the barriers
> within yourself that you have built against it."*

> *"Taking our hearts and looking them in the face is the essence
> of the wilderness experience."*

In the "wilderness" of this time, HE is graciously letting me look
at my heart and see all those places where I resist or have
barriers to His love. The reality is that we live in His love. It (as
the Psalmists say over and over) endures forever. It permeates all
and is present in all, and we receive it as we awake from those
barriers that keep us asleep.

13

Good, Good Father

One of the songs that became a kind of theme song for me during these days was *Good, Good Father*. My spiritual director introduced me to the song and it was on repeat many days. I distinctly remember driving to the hospital in the early morning hours, still dark outside, and blaring this song as I turned into the parking lot. I was about to have a fairly invasive surgical biopsy and tears flowed as I declared that He is a good father to me. During early days of chemotherapy when I would wake in the middle of the night, one line from this song ministered to me deeply:

> *Oh, I've heard a thousand stories of what they think you're like, but I've heard the tender whisper of love in the dead of night. And you tell me that you're pleased and that I'm never alone.*

By His grace, I was living in a place of not trusting in stories but resting in His tender whisper of love. In pain, awake at two in the morning, I found myself surrounded by His love. In so many ways, I felt like I was not just believing things but experiencing them. It is one thing to know that God loves you and it is another thing to know it because you have heard it in the depths of your soul.

I had an experience while in the hospital months earlier in that year that felt like a tender whisper. I had to have a lumbar puncture on four occasions. A lumbar puncture is a procedure in which a doctor inserts a needle into your spine. For my treatment, I had to get a regular biopsy of the spinal fluid because leukemia, apparently, likes to hide out there. So, the doctor would take a biopsy and then inject the spine with some chemotherapy for good measure. It is a bit of an understatement but that was not a fun time. In fact, even though they would give several injections of lidocaine before the big needle went in, the doctor was often having to navigate nerves and when nerves were hit by the needle, I would feel a painful electrical sensation down one of my legs. For subsequent lumbar punctures, the docs would have to also navigate scar tissue from the previous punctures. I usually had to have a talk with doctor about where to put in the needle and what my history had been with the punctures.

The first time I was taken into the room for this procedure there was a nurse who held my hand while the needle was going in for biopsy and then the injection of chemo. In that moment, it felt like God was holding my hand. She told me that she wasn't usually in that procedure room. And, then, the next time I went for a lumbar puncture, that same nurse was there. She said she had been floated there again from another unit. I sensed deeply that God was saying, "I'm here. I've got you."

And, then, for my third lumbar puncture, again – she "happened" to be there on assignment from another department. That procedure I remember as being especially painful and she was there. I wondered if perhaps she was an angel but what I did know is God used her (perhaps outside her awareness) to communicate His love, provision, and presence to me. I felt loved and cared for by the God of the Universe, who also happens to be a good Father.

Knowing that we have a good Father means that we can trust His love, provision, and presence. That's why no matter the specifics of the storm we are in, we can expect to hear that tender whisper that He is lovingly present with us.

In Matthew 7, Jesus talks about the goodness of the Father and uses the analogy of an earthly father and son. "If he asks for fish, he won't give him a snake, will he?" The answer is clear: of course not. Because of this, we can enter into anything with a "yes."

We can say yes.

We can look for His good presence in every situation.

This doesn't mean that we aren't real about things that are hard. It does mean that God's presence with us in all things opens us to seeing Him and seeing the ways that He is at work. If He is good, we can trust. Really. We can trust.

Often when we hear the word discernment, we think about making decisions. However, in the history of God's people, it has more often referred the practice of discerning God's heart and activity in our lives. Of course, this can have an impact on decisions but rather than thinking about it in terms of making good decisions, it is better to think about it in terms of being attentive to God, what He is doing, and how He is with us.

In John 5:19, Jesus makes the statement that He only does what He sees the Father doing. That is discernment. Because God is good and He is present with us, we can approach everything, even the hard things, with a sense of anticipation. It's as if we can say: *Okay, God, what are you up to? How are you present with me in this?* We can look for His love.

The Scriptures are full of descriptions of how He is with us and what He does. One of the most compelling is in Zephaniah 3:17 where we are told:

> *The Lord your God is in your midst, a mighty one who will save; he will rejoice over you with gladness; he will quiet you by his love; he will exult over you with loud singing.*

Knowing this, trusting this, we can move into our lives looking for the gifts, the little winks from God that He is with us and loving us. They are there. However, we have to look. The Persian poet Rumi wrote, "Your task is not to seek love, but merely to find all the barriers within yourself that you have built against it." What barriers do we put us that keep us from discerning His love? Can you open your heart to seeing His love in the midst of suffering? Can you slow down enough to notice? Do you want relief more than experiencing His love? Pray and ask God to help you lay aside anything that might be a barrier.

In the month after month of treatments, tests, surgeries, and hospitalizations, I was able to see God's love over and over again. By His grace, God had been building in me an ability to see Him and discern Him. There are indeed thousands of stories but I'll share two. Both come from my kids.

My first year of treatment was during my son Trey's senior year of high school (I was completely bald at his graduation!). Every day, Trey would go out of his way and ask me how I was feeling and how I was doing. He genuinely cared for and loved me. I was stunned as I looked at this young man who I had held in my arms as a baby now holding me close and attending to me as I laid in bed unable to do things I normally did to take care of him. As I write these words, tears are my coming to my eyes because what father gets to have his teenage son express such compassion and love? What a gift God gave me!

During my daughter Claire's junior year of high school, I was hospitalized for over 3 months. Most days, she visited me and many of those days, especially when I was at my weakest, she would get up in the hospital bed with me. Like Trey, this young woman who I held as a baby was now holding me, comforting me. Again, what a gift for my daughter to love me and express such tenderness. I thank God that I was able to see it and experience it as His love through her.

These are memories that have been permanently imprinted in my soul. He is actively loving us every minute because He is a good, good Father. Are you discerning that love? Are you noticing?

Tuesday, April 2   **New Timeline and News**

Because of scheduling with the donor in Germany, the date of the transplant has changed. I will now be admitted to the hospital for 6 days of chemo on April 12 and the transplant will be on April 19. Tears came to my eyes last night when I realized that the 19th is Good Friday, that day when one person offered their blood/their life so that we may live. I am going to get to experience this reality in a very physical, tangible way. More than that - it feels like a reminder from our gracious God that He is in this, He has this.

I also found out yesterday that the donation is anonymous from both sides. I can send an anonymous letter but that's it. Then, after 2 years, there will be the choice to release information. A big request from my heart right now is that you might pray for the donor, I thank God for what the donor is doing and I also pray that he would experience God in this ... that his heart would be drawn to Jesus in a new, refreshing way.

I have a friend who gave me a snow globe type of thing in which two penguins are just floating on top of the water. If you give it a shake, waves crash over the penguins. I am reminded of the analogy that we often flail against the water as we are thrown into the deep, forgetting that we can simply float. My prayer in these days ahead is that I would simply float ... resting in the reality of His goodness, provision, and grace ... resting in the truth that He is holding me up.

Thursday, April 11   **Stem Cell Transplant, here we go!**
Just a quick email to thank you for your prayers as I enter the
hospital tomorrow for about a month. I'll have 6 days of chemo
that will prepare my bone marrow to receive the new stem cells
next Friday. It is a process of my body **releasing** the old immune
system and old stem cells so that I can **receive** the new ones.

My prayer is that I am able (in body, mind, and spirit) to release
so that I can receive this gift. Pray for that. I believe that I am
ready but I am deeply aware that this is a whole-body
experience.

I am going to be praying through and meditating on Psalm 46
in the coming weeks and month. The Psalm which is most
famous for verse 10 ("Be still and know ...") begins with a verse
that talks about God's abundant presence. The result? In verse
two, "therefore, we will not fear." My prayer is that there is no
fear, no-thing that would be a barrier to receiving all the gifts in
this experience (including the cells themselves) because I am
resting in His good presence.

Love you all ...

Thursday, April 18   **New Life, Good Friday, and Easter**
Well, here we are ... during this Holy Week of Good Friday and
the Resurrection. I am humbled and overwhelmed by the
opportunity to receive new life on Good Friday. Someone giving
their blood for me ... anonymously. How gracious. Jesus shed
His blood for me long before I had an inkling that He had done

so. In a sense, He gave anonymously - waiting in vulnerability for the day when I would open the gift and receive, trusting what He did for me.

As my blood counts drop, I am feeling weaker and more vulnerable but this is part of the process of my body getting ready to receive. I am reminded that the Lord graciously takes us to weakness so that we can receive what we never would otherwise. I am also reminded that the greatest gifts of this whole process will not be physical life extended but deeper life in Him infused into me. For that I am so grateful.

The transplant is Friday morning at 9:30 and should last anywhere from 1-2 hours. We got a report this morning that the collection of the donor's stem cells went really well and they are in transit right now. I invite you to pray in the morning the following blessing for the transplant. We also have a small group of family praying this in the morning at the hospital:

Most Merciful God, Creator, and Sustainer of Life,

We come before you today, humbled by your great gift of life. In your infinite love, you planted within us these tiny cells that have the power to heal and renew. For giving scientists, physicians, and nurses the knowledge to use these cells for our well-being, we give you thanks. For having brought us to this special day, we give you thanks. Today, we ask a special blessing on Ted as he receives these life-giving cells. Let him trust not only in their power to heal, but in Your invitation to new life and new birth. Grant Ted patience and hope as he waits for the restoration of body, mind, and spirit.

And now, send you Spirit upon these cells, blessing them with your love and healing power.

In Your holy name, we pray, Amen.

Friday, April 19 **Quick Update**

All went well with the transplant today! Thanks for all your prayers and notes of encouragement.

Now, we just wait while the new stem cells engraft. This will take a few to several weeks, and we're praying that there are not any complications. We are so grateful ... much love to you all.

Tuesday, April 23 **Day +4 Update**

Hi Friends - my days are presently being measured with last Friday being Day 0. Today is Day +4 and I wanted to give a quick update. After receiving my new stem cells last Friday, we are now waiting for all of my blood counts to go down so that the new cells can take over. As my counts go down, my fatigue increases and my GI tract suffers. I am feeling ok today but feeling the drift to the harder days. On average, Day +18 is when new blood counts start rising because of the new cells. It can take longer or even a few days less. So, I appreciate your prayers ... that things would go smoothly and on schedule. I'd love that!

More so, pray that I will stay present to the day. It is so easy to drift into thinking, "I can't wait to get out of here" or simply let my mind and heart focus on what is next rather than what is right here, right now. There are so many opportunities to be present to Him ... so many people coming in and out of my room to whom I can show love and honor. I don't want to miss any of that because I am focused on me. At the same time, I need to make sure that I am being faithful to resting as much as possible and doing the things I can to present my body and soul to this process of healing.

I read this today and it was such an encouragement:

> *"Jesus talked about fears people have. And He dismissed all of them. You are an undying, eternal soul. If you will place yourself in the hands of God, there is nothing that can happen to you that will make you say, 'I do not have enough.' You don't have to fear anything." (Dallas Willard)*

It seems to me that staying present to the moment is the way that I place myself in His hands.

Friday, May 3   **Unbelievable News - Day 14**
I am amazed. Today is Day 14 and I am now home. There were lots of rough days over the last few weeks but my blood counts are going up which is showing that the new stem cells are engrafting. If you remember, Day 18 was the day we were hoping to see my counts up so this is incredible.

Thanks for all your prayers and notes and encouraging texts. The medical and nursing staff have been excellent to get me where I am. Now, I have the long recovery process ahead. Lots of rest each day, about 13 medications twice a day, and limits to my activity outside the house. I'll have 2-3 appointments at the hospital each week to monitor the progress and check medication levels, etc. All these things are welcomed because they are a part of the process.

Right now, I have so many thoughts in my heart and mind right but for now, let me just say Hallelujah ... one of my favorite Hebrew words made of 3 words: Halle (praise), lu (to) and jah (Yahweh). Even if I wasn't doing this well and was still in the hospital- I would be singing Hallelujah but today is a special kind of Hallelujah.

Thursday, May 16   27

Quick update from Jen....

Today is day +27 since Ted's stem cell transplant. Overall, he is doing as expected. But he was readmitted to the hospital last night with a blood clot in his neck. This is most likely from the central line catheter that he still has in his chest. He is on a blood thinner and will be in the hospital for a few days. Ted is disappointed and feels like this is a set-back, but the reality is there is nothing he did to cause the blood clot.

On a happier note, today Ted and I celebrate our 27th anniversary! Like true romantics we are celebrating in the hospital. But I can't think of anything more loving than to stick with one another on this journey.

We continue to find God's goodness in each day. Thank you for your support, encouragement and prayers and for journeying with us. We are so grateful for and appreciate each one of you!

Sunday, May 19 **Home**

Well, after 4 days in the hospital, I am back home. It is so good to sleep in a comfy bed and just have the comforts of home. I will be on a blood thinner for a while as the blood clot resolves, hopefully. Thanks for all your prayers and encouragement.
I so appreciate your continued partnering with me on this journey. The last couple of weeks have not been easy and the first few days in the hospital were hard. I was not expecting it and I realized how much that expectation was coloring my mood and ability to stay present to what was before me. The Lord graciously ministered to my heart and reminded me that this is how I am serving Him right now. I need not skip ahead to a time when I am feeling better and not at the hospital 4 times a week but this is my assignment in loving Him right now. My life is not my own ... my body is not my own. Pray that I would live in that reality!

Thursday, May 23 **Back in the Hospital**

I'm being admitted to the hospital again this afternoon as my GI issues are not resolving and my kidney function is off. They want to monitor things more closely than they can in an outpatient setting. In addition, I will have the endoscopy and colonoscopy tomorrow which were delayed because of the blood clot last week. They will take biopsies which will confirm that I am dealing with graft versus host disease. We've been told that this is not unusual but they want to deal with it all quickly so things don't progress.

Overall, I am encouraged to have such good care and look forward to treatments that can address the GI issues I'm experiencing. Again, I am seeking to remember that this is my context for loving Him and serving Him right now.
Pray that things are resolved smoothly and that my stay isn't long. Pray for continued wisdom for the docs. Pray for my heart to rest in Him.

Thursday, May 30   **Update from the hospital**
Friends and family, it is day #8 in the hospital (this time around) and I will be here through the weekend, at least. The biopsies taken last week confirmed Graft-Versus-host-Disease (GVHD) in my gastrointestinal tract. GVHD is pretty common and happens about 50% of the time. Because of this I am not able to eat, so I am receiving fluid nutrition through my IV. Medication and rest to my GI tract should slowly improve things. It will probably take 1-2 months for my GI tract to recover. The good news is that my lab results are improving and the stem cells have successfully engrafted.

Of course, please continue to pray for physical healing. And pray that my pain will be minimal (GVHD causes severe abdominal cramping). As always and more importantly, pray for my heart - that I will release my expectations and rest in His plan for me right now. I realized earlier this week that this setback and unexpected hospitalization threw me for a loop. The Lord graciously met me in this place and has been ministering to me. It is so easy to let expectations and plans rule us, and He is taking me into deeper places of emptying myself of my plans, expectations, etc.

Friday, June 7   **New Treatment & More Hospital Time**
Today marks day 15 in the hospital this time. The treatments for Graft vs. Host of my GI tract haven't worked so it has felt like 1 step forward and two steps back. Because the issues hadn't resolved themselves with the normal treatments - I am moving into a new treatment in which I will have my blood "filtered" twice a week to kill off the cells that are attacking my gut. Previous treatment involved steroids which addressed things more broadly. This treatment will be very specific as I'll be hooked up to a machine which will take out certain cells and medicate them using a process called "photopheresis." The side effects will be minimal and the docs are optimistic.

I will be in here through at least the weekend. I am doing well (feeling better physically each day) and my heart/soul are experiencing new levels of rest in His goodness and provision. I read this today and it resonated deeply:

> *"Say 'yes' to life on the terms that God is giving you life just now; pay attention to your life." Br. Curtis Almquist, SSJE*

Will you pray that with me? That I will continue to pay attention to this life He has for me right now and not put my heart on anything else. I want to say "yes" each day and as a result, love God by looking at His heart and love others because there is a hurting world around me that needs to know His heart for them.

Much love to you all. So thankful for the partnership you have with me in this ... I couldn't be more thankful!

14

Living in the Present Moment

One of the most difficult things in the world is to *stay present* ... present to and aware of that which is right in front of us. Our minds wander to considering how we will respond to what we are experiencing, to something in the past that relates to what we see, or to the future and what we are going to do later in the day or next year. Our cognitive ability is one of the gifts of being human, being able to consider the past and the future. This is what helps us make plans, build things, and learn quickly. We are able to categorize and assimilate information quickly based on past experiences. However, these abilities can make it difficult to stay tuned in to the present moment.

Why do we need to stay present to the moment? Primarily, because we are designed for and most satisfied in life in the context of relationship. Relationships are experienced in the present moment. Love happens in the present moment. Of course, we might love things that happened in the past or love the idea of a vacation in the future, but this is the loving of an idea or a concept. Loving relationally happens in the here and now.

So, the realm in which we can know and love God is in the present moment. Some have observed that God lives in the eternal now. Because God exists outside of time, He is always present. Our desire to know Him and experience Him demands that we grow in our ability to *be* in the present.

As we walk through the storms of life (including a serious illness), a significant temptation lies in the area of just wanting to move out of the present moment. For me, sometimes I found that my mind would drift to when I would get out of the hospital or when things would get better. From time to time, I'd move into thinking about when I used to be able to certain things that now were out of reach. So, we might dwell on "happier times" in the past or we fantasize about what things will be like when things are over. All the while, God is with us and loving us and we can miss it.

Jean Pierre de Caussade shared:

> The present moment holds infinite riches beyond your wildest dreams but you will only enjoy them to the extent of your faith and love. The more a soul loves, the more it longs, the more it hopes, the more it finds. The will of God is manifest in each moment, an immense ocean which the heart only fathoms in so far as it overflows with faith, trust and love. The whole of the rest of creation cannot fill your heart, which is larger than all that is not God; terrifying mountains are mere molehills to it. It is in his

purpose, hidden in the cloud of all that happens to you in the present moment, that you must rely. You will find it always surpasses your own wishes.

Say yes to the present moment.

And, how do we do that? Psalm 46 gives us an amazing picture of what it looks like to walk into *presence*. In verse 10, we read, "Be still and know that I am God." The context reveals that the psalmist was dealing with a world that felt like it was falling apart. He imagined the mountains falling into the sea. For the ancient people of God, mountains represented strength and the sea was a place of fear. So, any notion of strength and security was disintegrating. In that context, we find the words, "God is our refuge and strength; a very present help in trouble." The second half of that verse could be translated, "abundantly present and a help in trouble." God is present, abundantly so, in the midst of our storms.

We "know" this God as we learn to be still. When our minds are fluttering around, distracted by the pain and confusion of our current situation, we are anything but still. Stillness. It means that we are learning to release fear. Indeed, that is the response in Psalm 46, "We will not fear."

The releasing of fear is a gift that gets cultivated and refined in a time of suffering. I can remember spending most of my life afraid that I would get cancer. My mom died of cancer. Both of my grandmothers died of cancer. An aunt died of cancer. My

list could go on and yours might even be longer. The word
cancer strikes fear deep. Now, with all that I've walked through,
I have very little fear. As I learned more and more how to stay
present, a less than preferable future doesn't hold my attention.
This was a process to be sure.

I am aware that I am now more likely to get cancer again
because of the treatments and previous history. As I write this,
the chances of the leukemia recurring are about 12% and if
recurring, there is 40-50% chance I won't make it. I feel no fear
as I write these words. Not because of anything in me, but
because I know. I know, in an experiential way, this God who is
abundantly present, and resting in that reality dispels fear. The
love and presence of God has a way of casting out fear. John
makes this clear in his first letter, "perfect love casts out fear."
As we stay present to love and see life through the lens of His
love, fear no longer has a claim on us. Not that fear doesn't pop
up from time to time, but it is not in charge.

So, that idea of the "mountains falling into the sea" shifts to a focus
on the love and presence of God as we embrace stillness. Blaise
Pascal, the mathematician and philosopher, made the observation
that "All of humanity's problems stem from man's inability to sit
quietly in a room alone." Certainly, this isn't simply an outer
stillness, but a stillness of heart. However, we usually move into that
inner stillness we develop an outer, physical stillness.

Often, when people are afraid or panicked, we simply encourage
them to take a deep breath. Why do we do that? As we take a deep

breath, our body begins to regulate. When we are fearful, it is very likely that we go into a "fight or flight" response. The "primitive" brain takes over in stress and fear in order to survive. We do have the gift of thought in which we can distinguish, discern, and decide but our bodies shut off this ability in stress because it takes too long. The idea is this: if a bear comes running toward you in the forest, you don't have time to think through a rational, reasoned response. You flee (most likely) or you might fight. What is adaptive and helpful with bears is not the best approach if we desire to *be in the present moment.* We have to be able to slow down and be still, and taking a series of deep breaths helps us calm down physically so that we can be present.

Then, we are able to release fear as our shaping reality. Thomas Keating, in *Invitation from God,* says: "The basic disposition in the spiritual journey is the capacity to accept all reality; God, ourselves, other people, and all creation as they are." So, as we breathe deeply, we can also breath in all reality, holding it with God in trust.

We have everything we need. Sometimes it takes losing everything to realize that you have everything: a God who is abundantly present and a help in trouble. In addition, sometimes it requires learning to take a deep breath.

Saturday, June 15   **Home and Healing**

Well, after 21 days, I was discharged from the hospital. I am
now doing the photopheresis (Graft vs Host treatment) as an
outpatient therapy. I go for a two-hour session this morning.
And, I am on IV nutrition each night in which I get sustenance
along with small meals that I am trying to increase each day. I
am noticing small improvements so thanks for those prayers.
And, I can't even begin to express how wonderful it is to have
Jenifer by my side. She is such an amazing advocate and
companion in this journey.

Please also pray for patience ... it will take a few months for this
to even out and for me to eat normally. As I type this, I feel His
nearness and pleasure. "Oh, taste and see that the Lord is
good." I am realizing that food is so often used metaphorically
in Scripture to remind us that He is our sustenance & I desire
so desperately to live in that reality. HE is enough, truly...
specifically HIS love.

Friday, July 5   **Day 77 (post-transplant) Quick Update**

Many have asked how things are going and so here's a quick
update of what's going on:

I am at Day 77 which means the 100-day mark is fast
approaching. 100 days is a significant marker as I should see a
lot of improvement and there will be tests to see if there are
cancerous cells in the bone marrow. I have a bone marrow
biopsy coming up on July 22 and I'm excited to see where we
are. Overall, I have been feeling great. Most days, I feel really

normal except for some fatigue. A prayer request is that I stay patient and rest well, not pushing myself. I need to rest because I am not 100% and healing means that I pay attention to my body even when my mind says, "go." I am still very limited in what I can eat as I heal from the Graft vs. Host Disease of the GI tract. Pray that I am patient as I introduce new foods and build up what I can tolerate. It can be frustrating to be eating bland foods when chips/salsa and tacos call my name frequently.

So, please do keep praying ... this healing is a journey and even past the 100 days, I'll be limited in what I can do and my immune system will be vulnerable for at least the next year ... meaning I'll wear a mask in public and have to be very careful. My heart is in a good place as the Lord keeps leading me into patience, slowness, and stillness - these are realities that I relish living into whether my current circumstances were present or not.

Wednesday, July 24   **Good News**
Friends and Family, I got the results of my Bone Marrow Biopsy from Monday and it showed no signs of the Acute Myeloid Leukemia!

It hard to express in words all that is going on my mind and heart. At the core seems to be gratefulness and awe. I am in awe of God's provision and healing touch in my life. I know that His plan is not always for healing and yet it seems to be for now. I am in awe and it is producing deep gratefulness in my heart. I've shared this with you before but Ignatius of Loyola wrote this as part of Spiritual Exercises:

> We should not prefer health to sickness, riches to poverty, honor to dishonor, a long life to a short life . . . Our one desire and choice should be what is more conducive to the end for which we are created.

This is where I want to continue to live whether I stay free of the cancer or if it returns. It is a place of deep joy and rest and comfort, because now more than ever I believe I can say that what I want most is to live in intimacy in with Him. I am also grateful because this means that I likely won't be leaving this earth any time soon. You might remember that last summer I was told I was in remission and then there was the relapse of Hodgkin's as well as the emergence of Leukemia. So, I am under no illusions but I'm finding that my heart isn't troubled. He has been showing me how to live for today "because I don't know what tomorrow may bring." I am also grateful for that because it is just the best way to live.

Next Monday is Day 101 and we meet with oncologist. We'll get the full report as well as some genetic results from the biopsy that will hopefully confirm that the cancer is indeed gone. We'll learn next steps in the recovery process. Even though the transplant seems to have taken root, there is still recovery from the transplant but it is going so well. A month ago, Graft vs. Host Disease of the GI tract was severe and now medication and treatment seems to have resolved things. I am now eating anything I want and have lots of energy. My immune system is rebuilding and that will take 6 months to a year so I wear a mask in public and have to be careful. With all of this I am also deeply grateful as this seems to be progressing so much more quickly than anticipated.

Again, thank you for your prayers and support. We've never once felt alone or unsupported. In God's mysterious providence, He chooses to use the prayers of His people to accomplish His heart & you've been a part of that. Please keep praying as I continue to recover and right now, please celebrate His goodness! Much love to you all!

15

Holding All Things Loosely

Jesus makes a simple but brilliant statement at the end of a discussion about anxiety: "Therefore, do not be anxious about tomorrow, for tomorrow will be anxious for itself. Sufficient for the day is its own trouble." James, the brother of Jesus, writes something very similar: "Come now, you who say, 'Today or tomorrow we will go into such and such a town and spend a year there and trade and make a profit' – yet you do not yet know what tomorrow will bring. What is your life? For you are a mist that appears for a little time and then vanishes. Instead you ought to say, 'If the Lord wills, we live and do this or that.'"

What both Jesus and his brother are getting at is simple, but not necessarily so simple to live. The point: you don't know and can't control the future; so, hold conceptions of and hopes for the future loosely. And, in living in the present moment as we release fear, we are put in a position to do just that. James fleshes this out a bit more and suggests an abandonment to God's will. God's will is His heart. And the idea with James as well as with Jesus is that we can trust God's heart.

Having been declared free of cancer four times and three times it has come back, I've moved into holding things loosely. It is not an easy process and it doesn't mean that I've given up or don't care. On the contrary, I've seen God shape my heart more fully into trusting God's heart and His vision for the future. Of course, part of the challenge is that we naturally want to know what the future holds and this can become the focus of our prayers. We want to know or at least we want assurances that all will be okay. As the great Oswald Chambers said, "Have you been asking God what He is going to do? He will never tell you. God does not tell you what He is going to do; He reveals to you Who He is."

God promises Himself, not glimpses into the future. Because God's will is His heart, He graciously prods us back to the present moment over and over again where we experience Him. Unfortunately, we may have been taught that God's will is something we can discover like being on a treasure hunt. If we find the map, we can have assurance of what lies ahead, how the terrain looks, and the best route from point A to point B. However, God never tells us to search for His will or to try to discover it. Indeed, He tells us who He is and that we can trust *Him* because His "will" is His heart. So, then, obedience to God's will is being responsive to Him, following Him. It is a relational reality.

The result of all of this is that we can hold all things loosely. When our desire and focus is God's heart which is all about life with Him, we are less worried or vexed about what may or may not happen. So, will my cancer come back? I can hold that loosely. Will I get through this? I can hold that loosely. Will I get to walk my daughter down the aisle? I can hold that loosely, too. These are important, good questions but they can be held loosely because they are not the point of my life. We may not know the all the details and duration of this life of love for God and others, but we can trust that He is holding it all. If we cling to this or that version of how life will or should work, it can lead us off point and out of the present.

As I've shared several times, Ignatius of Loyola wrote these incredibly challenging and helpful words in his Spiritual Exercises:

> *We should not prefer health to sickness, riches to poverty, honor to dishonor, a long life to a short life . . . Our one desire and choice should be what is more conducive to the end for which we are created.*

The end for which we are created. Let's stay with that for a moment. My end? My purpose? My goal? Simply put: a life of love with the God of the universe. As I am able to return to that over and over again, a centeredness emerges and deepens in my life. And this is a gift not just in times of suffering but in all of life. When I can't be swayed by honor or dishonor, riches or poverty, I am free.

Free.

Holding all things loosely means that I am free to experience anything (sickness, health, poverty, riches, long or short life) and therefore, nothing can define me, nothing can move me away from this centeredness, nothing can shape me ... except Him. Indeed, this is what is discussed in Romans 12:

> I appeal to you therefore, brothers, by the mercies of God, to present your bodies as a living sacrifice, holy and acceptable to God, which is your spiritual worship. Do not be conformed to this world, but be transformed by the renewing of your mind, that by testing you may discern what is the will of God, what is good and acceptable and perfect.

We come back to this theme again: as we release our clinging and holding on to things, we are free to notice and discern His will (His heart) in all things. In the Beatitudes, Jesus said: "Blessed are the pure in heart, for they shall see God." (Matthew 5:8) The pure in heart are those who "desire one thing." My desire is no longer focused on being healed or living pain free or having certainties. My desire centered on Him.

None of this is easy. There may be moments of grace when it is, but more often it requires a settled intention to release and let go of expectations and preferred outcomes. For me, I found over and over again that I had to be intentional. When I felt emotions pushing me to cling and hold on, I had to notice the emotions and listen, with God, to what they were revealing. I cried more in these years than I had in the previous 47 years combined. I cried at commercials of a dad walking his daughter down the aisle. I cried when I felt the uncertainty of it all. I cried when I had to call my dad and tell him the cancer had come back again. My list could go on, but what I found was that listening and responding to my emotions rather than shutting them down or letting them direct my course was vital. As I listened to them, I was able to affirm the good desires they revealed and I was able to release the lesser (or sometimes, unhealthy) desires. Thomas Keating, in *Invitation to Love*, gives us some insight:

> As we begin the difficult work of confronting our own unconscious motivations, our emotions can be our best allies. The emotions faithfully respond to what our value system is – not what we would like for it to be, or what we think it is. Our emotions are perfect recorders of what is happening inside; hence they are the key to finding out what our emotional programs for happiness really are.

And so, we notice our emotions, identify the motivation, release expectations and preferred outcomes, and redirect our desire. When we release, then we redirect our desire for health or riches (or whatever else) toward nurturing our desire for God alone.

As we do this, we are flexing a spiritual muscle ... the "releasing muscle" that gives space for freedom, peace, and joy. In the development of any muscle, strength is developed over time. And, as this muscle is developed, we hold things loosely.

Thursday, August 15 **Update from the Treatment Room**

As I type this, I am at the hospital receiving treatment for Graft vs. Host Disease. The good news is that it seems to be under control and I am experiencing no symptoms. In addition, I feel amazing ... very little fatigue (which I had thought would be an issue for 6-12 months) and I am working at almost 100%. The docs are reducing my medications week by week. I came home from transplant with about 25 medications to take daily and am now down to about 15 (and many of them are smaller doses). I was very weak when I returned home and could barely make it one block down the street, and now I am walking 2 miles a day. I still have a ways to go in getting my strength back but am making significant strides. The doctors are encouraged and are mainly monitoring my progress and managing the medications and treatments.

The main issue right now is being careful with the fact that my immune system is not built back up yet. So, I wear a mask when I am in public which will be the case for at least the next six months. It's a small price to pay to stay healthy but I feel so good that I often forget that I still have a ways to go. I am still very vulnerable even though I don't feel like I am. 1 in 5 people don't make it through this process from beginning to end and while things look very positive, I need to stay in that place of dependent trust.

Thanks for your continued prayers as I am in this healing and recovery process. Pray that I am wise with my recovery and continue to be careful. Please also pray that I stay with the things that the Lord led me through in my time in the hospital.

Primary among them is that reality of vulnerability. I don't want to get back to "normal" if normal means that I think I'm strong and invulnerable. I have a friend in his eighties who has shared with me that the great thing about growing old (if you have the spiritual sensibility to see it this way) is that you are no longer under the illusion that you can control life.

Wednesday, September 11　　　　　　　**In the hospital**

Hey everyone, as always – thanks for your prayers and encouragement. I am in the hospital with pneumonia. I came in on Sunday afternoon, straight from the airport. I had a high fever and as a bone marrow transplant patient, I have to be very careful with that. So, please pray for healing. It took them a couple of days to diagnose pneumonia and then a bronchoscopy to diagnose the kind of pneumonia. I am now on a new antibiotic which should do the trick.

My heart is good. I'm in a good place. I definitely sense the Lord's presence and pleasure and purpose in all of this. He's ministered to me in deep places during these days and I am so grateful. It will sound crazy but if a hospital stay is what it takes to continue to go deeper – I'll do it.

I just want to abide in him! Please pray for that.

Wednesday, October 9　　　　　　　**Quick Update**

I am now almost 6 months post stem cell transplant and I am feeling great. I still have a way to go with my immune system and my physical stamina but when the oncologist asked last week if there was anything bothering me or if there was anything I wish I could do, "I said no." Of course, I hope to eat sushi again someday and would love to run a marathon but those things will come in time and if not, it is okay. I'll have a scan every three months in this first year and a blood test monthly to check that I am still cancer free. And, I am still going to the hospital at least once a week for other blood tests, maintenance of my central line (still in my chest), treatments for graft vs. host disease, and other appointments to manage side effects of all that I've done in the last two years but it is all part of the journey and I find myself grateful to get to do these things. In the scope of human history, it wasn't long ago (30 years) that I likely wouldn't be alive right now so visits to the hospital right now are joyful reminders that I am alive.

So, I won't be posting a lot here in the coming months unless there is some excitement and there could be. Set-backs in the first year are common and recurrence of disease isn't uncommon either. However, I find myself in a deep place of peace. He has carried me through deep waters and I know He'll do the same if more excitement comes my way.

In it all, I just want to abide in all His love. Over the last few months, I have been reflecting on a verse from Jude that simply says "keep yourselves in the love of God." That is it. That is my deepest desire. We love because He first loved us" (1 John 4) and then He invites us into that love, "love the Lord and your neighbor" (Matthew 22).

The Lord has graciously removed so many barriers to love over the last couple of years and I do not want to put any back up. In fact, I desire to keep any barriers flattened by His grace. There are so many things that I seek to clothe me and I am reminded that it is His love alone that is my perfect clothing: "clothe yourselves in love." (Colossians 3:14) Will you pray that with me? That each day, we allow barriers to drop so that we experience His love as enough. His love alone is the perfect fit.

Wednesday, November 27   **Coming Full Circle**
Well, here we are: it is a day before Thanksgiving and I am certainly filled with gratitude. It was two years ago today that I had a port placed in my chest at the hospital and then went to the cancer clinic to receive my first dose of chemotherapy. On Monday of this week, I had a central line catheter (the sixth such port or line I've had in my body over the last two years) removed! Last Friday, I finished six months of treatment for graft vs. host disease which utilized that central line for treatment of my white blood cells. So, it was time to take out the catheter.

I can now take a shower without having to wrap my chest with cling-wrap and surgical tape. Sounds like a small thing, and it is, in the grand scheme of things, but it is symbolic that life is getting back to normal. My oncologist says that they will start weaning me off of some of the meds I am on as well. So, if feels like I've come full circle ... I realize that I am not out of the woods but it feels like I'm standing on the edge of the woods -

looking out over the wide-open space of a large meadow and taking in the warm sun that is in short supply when in the deep woods. I am not in the clear because chances of recurrence of the cancer in the first year after transplant are 20% but I am enjoying each day, not worrying about the future. Jesus has been holding me close over these last years and I know He will continue to do so ... whether I am plunged back into the woods or if I continue to walk out into the wide-open spaces.

As always, thanks for your prayers ... I am feeling so good right now. I haven't felt this good since August 2017. You can pray for continued healing and good health but even more, please pray that I would abide in His love - that's all I truly care about. I believe that most of the time and when I don't - I trust that it is true deep down in my soul.

I have a CT Scan next week to check on the lymphoma and will probably have a bone marrow biopsy after the first of the year to check on the leukemia.

Tuesday, December 3   **Good News**

Just a quick update: I had a full CT Scan today and it came back clear. Wow! This afternoon, I saw the email from my oncologist and clicked on it with anticipation ... wondering if it was back to the drawing board or moving forward. Well, we continue to march forward and I'm grateful. I almost can't believe it. God is so kind and merciful. I am humbled. Humbled that I am in this place and humbled to have friends like you who care and pray.

Tuesday, April 29   **Drum Roll Please ...**

... and all the year one tests show no evidence of cancer (no recurrence of lymphoma or leukemia). Thank you, Lord.

On **one level**, it is that simple - I am in a really good place. I met with my oncologist for an hour this morning & CT scans, Bone Marrow Biopsy, and blood tests were all great. She said that I am doing really well. I have 100% donor cells in my bone marrow which makes all the blood in my body.

Now, the delicate process of managing and reducing medications. I still have Graft vs. Host Disease and anemia (low hemoglobin and platelets) as well as a blood clot in my arm that emerged last week. That's the **other level**. But let me tell you - these are very small issues in the grand scheme of things.

One of the other things I talked to my doc about today was that 80% of people that go through a transplant experience PTSD, and starting to deal with some of these issues happens around the one-year mark after transplant. In addition, I had over a year of chemo, surgeries, and treatments (and a different cancer) before the leukemia and transplant. So, I appreciate your prayers for me physically and also emotionally. I shared with my doc today (and I'm going to be very transparent here) that one of the things I deal with is life is not as intense and exciting as going through all the treatments. "Normal" life can feel a little flat and even boring. It sounds weird and I even told her that and she looked at me and said, "that is very common." We used the war analogy to talk about the stress and drama of war, and how soldiers entering back into normal life (as much as it is desired) feels flat. So, thankfully, I've been processing a lot of things and will continue but it has not been easy to name and navigate the feelings and emotions.

I feel like I could share so much because there is deep joy in all of this and what I want to say to you all, my team that has been praying, is thank you. (those two simple words don't seem adequate but it is what we have!) Thank you for caring about me and reading these blog posts. For now, I'll shut this down and you won't see more updates from me. One of the gifts in all of this is that I'm not afraid - I'm not afraid of it coming back, I'm not afraid to get sick again, I'm not afraid to die. I feel like I'm "playing with house money" and have nothing to lose.

The truth is that I've never had anything to lose and I've never needed to be afraid but difficult things strip away illusions, if we let them, and plunge us deeper into reality ... the reality that there is a God who hold all things, including my life. I have nothing to prove, nothing to protect, nothing to possess - He holds it all and always has. For this I am beyond grateful. I pray that I am able to live deeper into these realities of "nothingness" - in John 3, John the Baptist said, "He must increase and I must decrease." The great German mystic Meister Eckhart wrote, "The soul does not grow by addition but by subtraction." By His great mercy, in a world that believes we need more and more and more, may I continue to let illusions die and my clinging to anything but Him decrease.

16

Subtraction, Not Addition

One of the things that drove me crazy (ok, maybe that's an exaggeration) as I walked through this journey is when people would ask me: "what are you learning?" Also, a bit frustrating was the statement: "I'm sure God is teaching you things so that you have something to share with others." People who asked questions and made statements like this meant well. I do appreciate their hearts. However, these kinds of sentiments may reveal a skewed understanding of what the spiritual journey in Christ is about. First, the idea that God takes us through hard seasons to teach us a lesson can sound punitive and unkind. Second, this idea can make it seem like our life in Christ is an intellectual pursuit ... the idea that we need new or different information. And, third, it may reduce life in Christ to a "growth" model. In other words, there is something I am lacking and suffering can provide what is lacking.

There is deep mystery surrounding God's sovereignty and human suffering. Theologians and scholars have debated and discussed the issue for centuries. The existence of a good God and the reality of human suffering present a tension that is beyond our ability to fully understand. The mechanics of it all are hard to comprehend, but I can tell you something that I know down deep in my bones: God graciously uses suffering in our lives. If we remain open to God, seasons of suffering can do something that seemingly nothing else can. It is not to teach us a lesson or help us grow spiritually, although those may be outcomes.

He allows us to be stripped of anything that isn't Him.

Meister Eckhardt, the German mystic of the 13th century, famously wrote: "The soul does not grow by addition but by subtraction." He strips us of all that we think we know and all that we believe we desire and in the empty space, we learn that He alone is all.

All.

He is all. Knowing Him is what we know. Desiring Him is what we desire. And, in that place of relational simplicity, there is a clarity and a purity that seemingly can come no other way. I've stopped trying to figure out the mechanics of it all and rest in the reality of a good God who *is*. He is. He exists, and as the writer of Hebrews so beautifully expresses, "Without faith it is impossible to please Him, for whoever would draw near to God must believe that He exists and that He rewards those who seek Him." The reward? Him. Undiluted, undistracted, unfiltered God. As we are busy about our normal lives, we frame God in certain ways. Perhaps in ways that fit our wants and preconceived ideas. But, walking through a time of suffering and hardship brings us to a place where we can see God on His own terms and it is beautiful.

Dr. Rachel Naomi Remen, an oncologist, states it well:

The view from the edge of life is different and often much clearer than the way most of us see things. Life-threatening illness may cause people to question what they have accepted as unchanging. Values that have been passed down in a family for generations may be recognized as inadequate; lifelong beliefs about personal capacities or what is important may prove to be mistaken. When life is stripped down to its very essentials, it is surprising how simple things become. Fewer and fewer things matter and those that matter, matter a great deal more.

The end, or goal, of a life rooted in Christ is relationship ... a relationship of intimacy. When we instead make it about lessons or growth (both important elements in our spiritual lives), we shift the goal to corollary things rather than life with Him, and in Him.

Having been in a hospital room, without earthly hope, suffering pain, fatigued both physically and mentally, I experienced the presence of God as a gift. Not by learning a new lesson, buy through subtraction, I saw the capacity of my soul expand. I was very aware that when all else seemed to evaporate, I was left with the love of God. And without the distractions and potential suitors for my trust, I found the love of God alone to be sufficient and actually beyond my understanding.

I bring us back to the prayer in Ephesians 3 in which we find a desire to comprehend that which is beyond understanding, the love of God which extends infinitely in all directions: height, width, depth, and length. The picture painted is that we are swimming in an ocean of love. And then, in Romans 5:5, we find that the Holy Spirit has poured this love into our hearts. God's love, all around us, and His love within us.

Perhaps, the greatest gift of suffering is indeed the subtraction, the loss. And, perhaps, that is why we don't even have to be afraid of loss because what seems like loss is actually great gain.

We can face our losses and traumas because we have come to know that in the midst of them, the presence and love of God is more real and palpable than ever.

Researchers have spent a lot of time over the last few years looking at the issue of trauma and loss. What we've learned is that when we experience trauma, our bodies tend to hold the trauma. There is a natural way that our brains process the events of daily life but with trauma we may bypass these regular systems. Normally, we integrate the events of life into the timeline of our lives. The pieces of our lives fit nicely into the story. With trauma, the pieces usually don't fit so nicely, so we hold them to the side. Our bodies catalogue and hold the experience.

Healing of the trauma we've been holding on to comes as we look at it and integrate it into the good story God is telling. Our small stories might not have space for the hard things but His story does.

Rachel Marie Martin echoes this theme:

> *Sometimes you have to let go of the picture of what you thought life would be like and learn to find joy in the story you are actually living.*

The story we are living is His good story. The loss of our story, our ideas of how life should go, can shift our focus to God's story as that which defines us and shapes us.

For me, without even fully realizing what I was doing, the blog where I wrote the facts and also integrated them into my life with God was a gift along the way. And then, these current reflections have even further put all the events of the last three years into the context of His story.

Along with your trauma finding space in your story, researchers have shared a few other practices that help with the subtraction that trauma brings. First, exercise helps. Sounds simple but trauma, being stored in your body, can wreak havoc and exercise keeps you breathing deeply and your blood pumping. Second, relational connections are key. In trauma, there is a tendency to isolate but we need listeners. We need people who are willing to listen to our story and give context. One of the powerful things about relationships is that they can keep us grounded. When I was in the hospital, I had some friends that would just show up and others, I would ask: *will you come and visit?* I wasn't asking because I felt sorry for myself or was lonely but because I needed connection with people I loved and trusted.

A life in Christ is not about adding or gaining, but subtraction as we learn to let go and release. From there, we rest ... rest in what is already true, rest in the reality that life is already complete and full in Christ.

If it seems that themes and subjects in what I have written keep repeating, that is by design. Perhaps, not so much my design but God's design. He gently, persistently, and patiently keeps reminding us of the same things over and over. And then He waits, He abides. Never demanding or over-powering us, He keeps whispering His grace which beckons us to a place of rest.

Final Thoughts: "Still Here, Papi"

When I was a child and into early adulthood, I would call my grandfather and the phone and ask him how he was doing. Almost without exception, he would respond with: "Still here, Papi." His first language was Spanish (and also the only language he spoke for most of the last year of his life) and Papi was a word he used in conversation as a term of endearment. In an almost a defeatist way, "Still here, Papi" expressed the idea that he hadn't died yet.

As I think about this, I am reminded: *I am still here.* Against some pretty significant odds and a long journey, I am still around. What has connected with me so deeply is that *someone* (hint, hint) must still want me around. I have walked up to the edge of death and looked it in the face a few times. I have accepted that fact that I could die tomorrow and I accept the reality of my own death. Indeed, I am mortal. Yet, the truth is that my life has never been my own and every second has been grace. I've finally come to a place where I can rest in that reality. Coming face to face with death and then continuing to live offers an amazing gift if we are willing to receive it.

For so many survivors of cancers, the question looms over their life, *what if it comes back?* This is a serious and difficult reality. When you make friends with your own death, you are able to hold that question without fear and even let it go. The Apostle Paul models this when he tells us it is far better to be with Christ, but also good to continue on with his brothers and sisters (Philippians 1:21-24). When you make friends with the fact that you are still here and your life is not your own, there is a freedom that money can't buy.

Teresa of Avila, talked about being in a place of prayer so sweet that she asked for the grace to die, and yet she saw that this was not God's will (heart):

> *I asked God for the grace to die so I could be with God in heaven. And I realized the only reason I was still alive is that it was God's will for me to be alive. Therefore, it is my desire to be one with God's will that I be alive, and when it is God's will for me to die, it will be my will."* (from her writings, shared in a podcast by James Finley about "The Interior Castle")

What if we lived in such a way that we were fully aware of our own mortality and saw every day as a gracious gift? I promise you that it will change you. It produces a lightness of being that is hard to explain. In the words of the old hymn, "The things of earth grow strangely dim in the light of His glory and grace." This dimness as we view earthly things doesn't produce an unhealthy detachment but a detachment that allows us to be in this world in non-anxious, non-possessive, and non-judgmental ways.

We all want to live that way, yet, often find it illusive. Suffering, and especially facing death, is able to give us that gift. And, we can all embrace such detachment as we face our own death. In Christ, we have the assurance that "Today, you will be with me in paradise." If you haven't ever come face to face with Christ and His promise, it is difficult to come face to face with death. But then, once we have, we can come back to the reality: *I'm still here.*

One of the brothers of the Society of Saint John the Evangelist in Cambridge, Massachusetts offer this word:

> *We don't possess our own lives. We are stewards of the life that God has given us, and for however long God continues to give us breath. Our life is not about hoarding or about conserving life for its own sake but its opposite: about giving. Our life is about our willingly giving up our life and our life's energies following the example we see in Christ's own self-emptying. (Curtis Almquist)*

You are still here.

If you are reading this, you are here and the gracious God of the universe has reasons for that. Every day is an adventure of discerning His love, discovering His purposes, and diving deep into the beauty that is life. You may be in a hospital room, on a ski slope, wondering how you will pay your next bill, or at work. Each moment, each day is an opportunity to be present, to be here.

> *The present moment holds infinite riches beyond your wildest dreams but you will only enjoy them to the extent of your faith and love. (Jean Pierre de Caussade)*

So, welcome everything.

REFLECTION GUIDE

As you read through these reflections, what are you noticing in your own soul? How might God be leading your heart? Are there ideas or concepts that you desire to embrace?

Consider the pattern of the Welcome Prayer from the opening pages ... welcome, let go, open ...

What are you being challenged to welcome?

What do you desire to release or let go?

How will you open yourself to God's love?

Whatever might be surfacing for you, talk to God about it. Hold your thoughts, ideas, feelings, or desires before Him, asking Him to lead your heart and your mind.

SPIRITUAL PRACTICES

As you read through *Welcome Everything*, you may find yourself interested in learning more about various spiritual practices that nurture and form our lives to be able to welcome everything.

On Ted's webpage, you'll find descriptions of the following practices (and maybe a few more as the list is updated over time):

- Centering Prayer
- Examen
- Lectio Divina
- Silence and Solitude
- Breath Prayer
- Rule of Life
- Spiritual Direction
- Community

Scan the QR code below to go to desertdirection.com/resources/spiritual-practices/

NOTES/REFLECTIONS

NOTES/REFLECTIONS

ACKNOWLEDGMENTS

It is not possible to accurately and adequately acknowledge all the wonderful people who were a part of the journey that is recorded and reflected upon in this book. However, I will try.

I am deeply grateful for all who prayed for me and with me in the years that I walked through my cancer journey. To those who sent emails, texts, cards, gifts, and gift cards as well as those helped us financially, I am still in awe of your love and encouragement. For those who visited me in the hospital and those who came and served me communion when I couldn't attend church, thank you.

I am thankful for my Emmaus community (Donnellys, Kelleys, and Robersons). I love you all so much. My community with the Spiritual Formation Society of Arizona supported me in so many wonderful ways. In the many months where I couldn't be present, our team lead the ministry so beautifully. The staff and community of Bethany Bible were a constant source of encouragement and practical support. There are way too many people to mention but my chemo angel, Vickie, has to top the list.

Grateful for my friends and co-laborers with Selah/LTI including the many interns with whom I get to serve and our beloved leader, Susan Currie. Phoenix Seminary supported me in so many ways, especially my friend and co-laborer John DelHousaye.

My spiritual director, Angela Wisdom, prayed with me and provided space for me to listen to God. Doug Kelley, who sat with me in the hospital more days than I can count or even remember, is a soul friend and fellow cancer journeyer. My dad and my brother were amazing in their care and constant contact. My dad called me every day to see how I was doing, even as he faced his own health challenges.

The doctors, nurses, PAs, and NPs who have taken such good care of me include so many that I can't even start to scratch the surface.

Mayo Clinic and Ironwood Cancer Center will always be holy places to me. Drs. Iyengar, Reeder, and Sproat will always be on my list of heroes as well as the whole hematology-oncology team at Mayo. The nurses of 7-West, 4-East, the ICU, the AIC, and the photopheresis unit ... I hope you know how much I love you.

Thanks to Ryan Brown for his great design work. And thank you to Michael Donnelly and Doug Kelley for reading and editing.

Trey and Claire, you've walked with me through some tough things. I was sick during some pivotal times in your lives (things like high school graduation, getting a driver's license, proms, homecomings, the beginning of college) and you never complained or asked why this was happening. You simply loved me and have become the most incredible young adults a dad could imagine. I love you guys and thank you for taking things seriously but never taking me seriously.

And, Jenifer, words could never suffice in expressing my grateful heart. You have certainly loved me in sickness and in health. When we got married, we vowed to be faithful in good times and bad, but we never thought about the bad. And, now, in amazing ways, even the "bad" times have been good. It has been in this season of sickness that I have seen the depths of your love and experienced your love in ways I could never have imagined back when I fell in love at first sight in high school. So thankful to God for bringing you into my life.

ABOUT THE AUTHOR

Ted Wueste is a spiritual director, pastor, author, and professor who lives in Phoenix, Arizona. Ted has served as a pastor for most of his adult life and now leads a spiritual formation ministry as well as teaching and writing. He is married to Jenifer and they have two adult children.

You can learn more about Ted at desertdirection.com where he blogs and shares resources. Scan the QR code below for a direct link:

Made in United States
North Haven, CT
21 August 2023